arizona's
BEST RECIPES

Featuring some of *Arizona Highways'* favorite restaurants

Editor: KELLY VAUGHN
Photographs: PAUL MARKOW
Designer: BARBARA GLYNN DENNEY
Copy Editor: NOAH AUSTIN
Photo Editor: JEFF KIDA
Editorial Assistants: NIKKI KIMBEL AND DEBORAH S. PADDISON

Library of Congress Control Number: 2014950946
ISBN: 978-0-9916228-4-9
First printing, 2015. Second printing, 2016. Third printing, 2016. Printed in China.

Published by the Book Division of *Arizona Highways* magazine,
a monthly publication of the Arizona Department of Transportation,
2039 W. Lewis Avenue, Phoenix, Arizona, 85009.
Telephone: 602-712-2200
Website: www.arizonahighways.com

Publisher: Win Holden
Associate Publisher: Kelly Mero
Editor: Robert Stieve
Senior Editor/Books: Kelly Vaughn
Associate Editor: Noah Austin
Creative Director: Barbara Glynn Denney
Art Director: Keith Whitney
Photography Editor: Jeff Kida
Editorial Administrator: Nikki Kimbel
Production Director: Michael Bianchi
Production Coordinator: Annette Phares

CONTENTS

CONTENTS

INTRODUCTION

Since 2008, *Arizona Highways* has published an annual *Best Restaurants* issue, so when it came time to create *Arizona's Best Recipes*, our editor, Robert Stieve, had an idea. It was natural to cull from the cream of the crop — the restaurants featured in the magazine over the years. Build the book from there, he said.

So we did.

After a little bit of planning, we reached out to our best restaurants and their chefs and owners. We told them about our hopes for a cookbook, and we asked for their favorite recipes. But we added a few criteria: The recipes need to be delicious, of course, but they also have to be simple enough for our readers to prepare in their home kitchens. And we hoped the chefs would be willing to let us send our 6-foot-4-inch-tall photographer into their kitchens to photograph each dish.

They agreed, we gathered recipes, and then we sent "Tall" Paul Markow across Arizona. After more than 6,000 miles, 35 restaurant visits and too many road meals to count, Paul came back with the images that appear on these pages. He calls the book his legacy project, and we're so happy he agreed to be a part of it. Paul, thank you.

Arizona's Best Recipes are wide-ranging, from Cliff Dwellers' New Zealand rack of lamb and the home fries at Matt's Big Breakfast to Garland's famous apple tart and Blue Buddha's yum-yum bombs. As you'll see, we've covered every corner of the state, as well as flavors for every palate.

Our thanks also go to the generous chefs who opened their kitchens and culinary brains to us. You'll find a complete list of the restaurants and their locations at the back of the book.

We hope you'll enjoy creating these meals for family and friends as much as you enjoy being served them in their respective restaurants.

Here's to happy eating.

For more information about Best Restaurants *and dining across the state, visit www.arizonahighways.com/eat-sleep.*

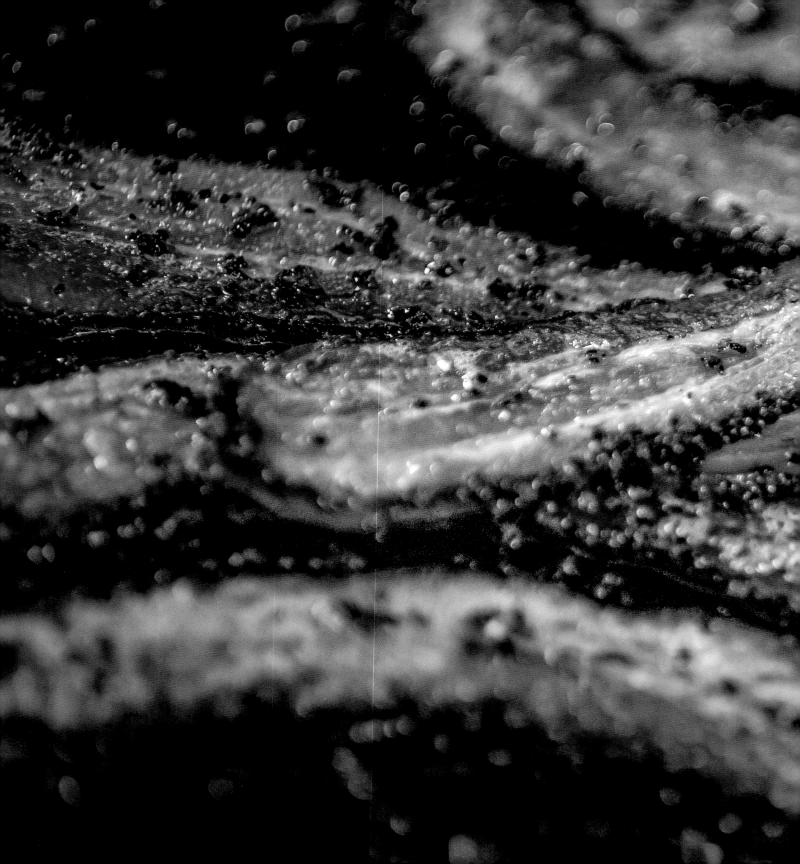

BREAKFAST

NANNY'S ZUCCHINI MUFFINS

The Randall House, Pine

[makes 12 muffins]

3 cups flour
1 + ½ cups sugar
1 teaspoon baking powder
1 teaspoon baking soda
1 teaspoon salt
1 teaspoon cinnamon
1 cup vegetable oil
½ cup milk
3 eggs
2 + ½ cups zucchini, grated
1 cup walnuts, chopped

Preheat oven to 350 degrees. In a medium bowl, stir together the flour, sugar, baking powder, baking soda, salt and cinnamon.

In a separate bowl, beat together the oil, milk and eggs, then add them to the dry mixture. Stir, then add the zucchini and walnuts.

Spoon the batter into greased muffin cups until two-thirds full. Bake for approximately 30 minutes or until a toothpick inserted into the center of a muffin comes out clean.

THE FIVE SPOT

Matt's Big Breakfast, Phoenix

[makes one sandwich]

1 high-quality artisan potato or challah roll
⅛ cup butter
2 cage-free eggs
¼ cup onions, diced
½ ounce extra-virgin olive oil
2 slices thick-cut peppered bacon
1 slice American cheese

Slice the roll in half and butter both halves with half of the butter. Cook the eggs in a skillet with the remaining butter until they're over-hard, breaking the yolks. Flip the eggs in the pan once to finish.

Sauté the onions in the olive oil until they're very soft and nearly caramelized. Place the bacon on the bottom half of the roll, then the eggs atop the bacon. Top with the onions and cheese. Place the top half of the roll and cover the sandwich briefly in the pan until the cheese is slightly melted.

SALAMI SCRAMBLE WITH HOME FRIES

Matt's Big Breakfast, Phoenix

[serves one]

¼ cup high-quality sopressata salami, sliced
  into matchsticks

⅛ cup butter, melted

3 cage-free eggs, beaten

Add the salami and the melted butter to a skillet and
cook over medium-high heat for about 2 minutes
until almost crispy. Add beaten eggs and stir together.
Continue cooking for 2 to 3 minutes, stirring
occasionally until eggs just begin to set, taking care not
to overcook them.

Plate with home fries and serve with buttered toast and
preserves on the side.

HOME FRIES

[serves 10 to 12]

5 pounds Yukon Gold potatoes

2 + ½ tablespoons extra-virgin olive oil

1 medium yellow onion, diced

½ teaspoon sea salt

½ teaspoon freshly cracked black pepper

3 or 4 sprigs fresh rosemary, stripped from stems

Preheat oven to 475 degrees.

Boil the potatoes in a large pot for 45 minutes. They
should be fork tender, but not mushy. Dice the
potatoes into approximately ½-inch cubes. Drizzle with
2 tablespoons of the olive oil, and roast for about
45 minutes until nicely golden brown.

Sauté the onion over medium-high heat with
the remaining olive oil until very soft and nearly
caramelized. Add the potatoes to a large skillet. Add
the salt, pepper, onions and rosemary, and sauté
together over high heat for 5 to 6 minutes until flavors
are blended well. Reduce heat to low, and hold until
ready to serve.

KEN'S BACON & SWISS QUICHE

Bisbee Breakfast Club, Bisbee

[serves four]

¼ cup Vidalia onions, finely diced
⅓ cup mixed bell peppers, julienned
¾ cup crispy bacon, chopped
9-inch unbaked pie shell
1 cup Swiss cheese, shredded
5 eggs
1 cup light cream
Pinch of nutmeg
Salt and pepper to taste

Preheat oven to 350 degrees. In a medium-sized mixing bowl, mix the onion, peppers and bacon, then layer them over the bottom of the pie crust. Sprinkle the cheese over the top of the mixture.

In a separate bowl, combine the eggs, cream, nutmeg and a pinch of salt and pepper. Beat until smooth and pour over bacon mixture. Bake for 40 minutes, turning 180 degrees halfway through.

Let cool for 10 to 15 minutes before serving.

BRIOCHE FRENCH TOAST WITH BANANA CARAMEL SAUCE

Essence Bakery Café, Tempe and Phoenix

[serves six]

8 large eggs
1 cup whole milk
1 cup heavy cream
1 loaf brioche bread, cut into thick slices

Crack eggs into bowl and whisk well. Add milk and heavy cream. Combine.

Dip brioche in egg mixture. Shake off excess egg mixture and place in buttered, non-stick pan over medium heat to lightly golden on both sides.

Top with Banana Caramel Sauce, fresh berries and toasted hazelnuts for garnish.

BANANA CARAMEL SAUCE

1 cup caramel sauce
1 large, ripe banana
¼ teaspoon ground cinnamon
1 teaspoon vanilla extract
2 tablespoons fresh lemon juice
2 tablespoons honey
½ cup simple syrup (boil ¼ cup sugar
    and ¼ cup water)

Combine all ingredients in food processor until smooth. Gently heat in microwave to serve warm with French toast.

SOUPS & SALADS

"EXOTIC" BEET SALAD

Cucina Rustica, Sedona

[serves two to four]

2 cups lettuce leaves (spring mix, butter lettuce or baby
  lettuce)
3 or 4 small beets
½ cup chèvre, crumbled

Preheat oven to 350 degrees. Toss greens with house
dressing (recipe below). Wrap the beets in foil and
roast them until fork tender, approximately 45 minutes.
Allow the beets to cool, then peel and slice into
quarter-inch pieces. Place lettuce on a serving platter
and arrange the beets on top. Sprinkle with crumbled
chèvre and drizzle with house dressing.

CUCINA RUSTICA
HOUSE DRESSING

¼ cup rice wine vinegar
2 tablespoons light soy sauce
¼ cup organic Arizona honey
Pinch of red chile flakes
2 pinches of salt, to taste
Pinch of black pepper, freshly ground
½ cup canola or light olive oil
½ teaspoon toasted sesame oil

Combine all ingredients, with the exception of the oils.
Whisk in olive oil in a slow stream, followed by the
sesame oil. Mix well, taste and add salt if desired.

MINESTRONE SOUP

Enzo's Ristorante Italiano, Snowflake

[serves four]

4 tablespoons olive oil

1 medium red onion, finely diced

4 cloves garlic, crushed

3 quarts water or chicken stock

2 red potatoes, peeled and diced in quarter-inch cubes

1 celery stalk, diced

4 medium mushrooms, diced

1 can cannellini beans (do not drain)

1 tablespoon granulated garlic

3 teaspoons black pepper

1 tablespoon salt

¼ cup Parmesan cheese, finely grated

½ cup Italian flat-leaf parsley, finely chopped

1 + ½ to 1 + ¾ cups marinara sauce
   (preferably homemade)

1 to 2 tablespoons basil pesto

¾ to 1 cup ditalini pasta

Place the olive oil in a 6-quart pot and add the onions. Sauté over medium heat until translucent, then add garlic. Continue to cook for an additional 3 to 5 minutes, stirring frequently to prevent burning.

Add the water and chicken stock and bring to a boil over high heat. Add the potatoes, celery, mushrooms and beans. Return the liquid to a boil, then reduce to medium-high heat.

Add garlic, black pepper, salt, Parmesan cheese and parsley. Simmer for 40 minutes, stirring occasionally.

Add marinara sauce and pesto and cook for an additional 15 minutes. Add the pasta and cook an additional 6 to 8 minutes.

For added robust flavor, add cooked ground sausage or pepperoni. Garnish with additional olive oil and Parmesan cheese.

FRENCH ONION SOUP

The Randall House, Pine

[serves 12]

5 pounds white onions, sliced
¼ cup olive oil
1 or 2 cloves garlic, chopped
2 tablespoons honey
3 tablespoons flour
3 quarts beef stock
2 bay leaves
½ teaspoon pepper, freshly ground
Melba toast
Swiss cheese
Fresh parsley

Preheat oven to 350 degrees.

Sauté onions in olive oil over low heat until they're translucent, approximately 20 minutes. Add chopped garlic and sauté an additional 2 minutes. Add honey. Continue to simmer until onions are golden, approximately 20 minutes.

Stir flour into the onions, then add the stock, bay leaves and pepper. Bring to a boil and simmer approximately 45 minutes.

Ladle soup into oven-proof serving bowls. Top with Melba toast and Swiss cheese. Bake for approximately 10 minutes or until the cheese has melted. Garnish with fresh parsley.

CIOPPINO

Gerardo's Firewood Café, Payson

[serves one]

2 tablespoons olive oil
2 ounces fresh fish
½ lobster tail
4 clams
4 mussels
3 ounces calamari, cut in rings
Pinch of red-pepper flakes
1 teaspoon garlic, chopped
1 teaspoon fresh herbs (basil, sage and parsley)

4 shrimp, cleaned and peeled
1 ounce white wine
½ ounce brandy
6 ounces tomato purée
1 teaspoon Tabasco sauce
1 teaspoon Worcestershire sauce
1 ounce butter
½ ounce tomato, diced

Pour the oil into a deep skillet and sauté the fresh fish, lobster, clams, mussels, calamari, red-pepper flakes, garlic and herbs until tender.

Add the shrimp, white wine, brandy and tomato purée. Cook on medium heat for 5 minutes. Add Tabasco, Worcestershire, butter and diced tomatoes.

EL TOVAR MEDITERRANEAN ENTRÉE SALAD

El Tovar Dining Room, Grand Canyon National Park

[serves four]

4 6-ounce boneless, skinless chicken breasts

¾ cup fresh baby spinach

¾ cup romaine lettuce, chopped

3 cups balsamic marinated chicken, grilled and sliced
(see note in directions)

¾ cup artichoke hearts, canned or jarred

24 Kalamata olives, pitted

⅛ cup sliced, roasted red peppers, canned or jarred

½ red onion, sliced

⅛ cup crumbled feta cheese

1 avocado, pitted, quartered and sliced

Marinate chicken breasts in El Tovar balsamic marinade (recipe below) for 24 hours. Drain and dry breasts, then cook on grill over high heat until an internal temperature of 165 degrees is achieved. Refrigerate chicken until cool, then slice into ¼-inch strips. Each breast will be one portion for each salad.

In a large bowl, combine spinach, romaine and 4 ounces of El Tovar balsamic dressing (recipe below). Mix thoroughly. Divide evenly among 4 large entrée plates.

Distribute equal amounts of artichoke hearts, olives, red peppers and red onion over each salad. Place sliced chicken breast in the center of each salad and top with crumbled feta cheese and a fan of one-quarter of an avocado.

EL TOVAR BALSAMIC DRESSING & MARINADE

2 cups balsamic vinegar

3 cups extra-virgin olive oil

1 quart cottonseed oil

½ ounce salt

⅓ ounce ground black pepper

½ ounce fresh garlic

⅔ ounce dried oregano

Place all ingredients in a blender and mix on high until emulsified.

CURRY CHICKEN SALAD

Sirens' Café, Kingman

[serves four]

1 roasted chicken, boned and diced
2 ribs celery, diced
1 bunch green onions, sliced
1 green apple, diced
½ cup dried cranberries
¾ cup whole salted cashews
2 tablespoons curry powder
1 + ½ cups mayonnaise
Salt and pepper to taste

Combine all ingredients and serve on wheat bread or a croissant as a sandwich, or with crackers or on a bed of greens as a salad.

HAM AND PEA SOUP

Sirens' Café, Kingman

[serves eight]

½ onion, diced
2 ribs celery, diced
3 large carrots, diced
½ cup butter
¼ cup ham, diced
4 cups chicken broth
4 cups milk
2 pounds frozen peas
1 + ½ teaspoons dried tarragon
Salt and pepper to taste
1 cup flour (optional)

Sauté onion, celery and carrots in butter for 15 minutes or until soft. Add ham and cook for an additional 5 minutes. Stir in broth, milk, peas and tarragon and simmer for approximately 20 minutes. Season with salt and pepper to taste.

For a thicker soup, add flour at the end. Start with a cup of flour in a small bowl. Add 1 cup of the broth of the prepared soup and mix until smooth. Whisk the flour mixture back into the soup and simmer for 5 minutes to thicken.

GREEN PAPAYA SALAD WITH CALAMARI

Rancho de los Caballeros, Wickenburg

GREEN PAPAYA SALAD

[serves four]

½ cup green papaya
⅛ cup bean sprouts
⅛ cup seaweed salad
¼ cup Napa cabbage, julienned thin
½ cup pickled ginger, julienned thin
8 leaves Thai basil, torn

Combine all ingredients, tearing the Thai basil leaves over the salad just prior to plating. Most ingredients can be purchased at an Asian-foods store.

CALAMARI

[serves six]

2 quarts frying oil
18 ounces calamari (squid)
½ teaspoon salt, to taste
Pinch of pepper, to taste
½ cup cornstarch
3 ounces cold water

In a 1-gallon soup pot, add the oil and heat to 350 degrees using an oil thermometer.

In a medium-size bowl, mix the squid, salt, pepper and cornstarch. Stir to incorporate, then add the water slowly and mix so the squid mixture is a thick-paste consistency.

Take the squid mixture in your hand and slowly break it up over the heated oil. To avoid being splashed with hot oil, do not drop the entire mixture into the oil at once.

Stir slowly to prevent the squid from sticking together. Cook for 3 to 4 minutes, then remove the calamari from the oil and allow excess oil to drain.

COCONUT CHICKEN SOUP

Dara Thai Café, Williams

[serves two to four]

4 to 6 slices galanga root
2 or 3 pieces lemon grass
3 to 5 kaffir leaves
½ cup coconut milk
½ cup chicken stock
½ cup chicken breast, sliced into small pieces
1 tablespoon chili jam (*nam prik pao*)
2 tablespoons fish sauce
1 tablespoon oyster sauce
2 tablespoons lemon juice
1 tablespoon sugar
½ cup mushrooms, sliced
Cilantro and chopped green onion for garnish

Boil the galanga, lemon grass and kaffir leaves in the coconut milk and the chicken stock. Add the chicken to the boiling soup and continue to boil for 7 minutes until the chicken meat is cooked completely. Add chili jam, fish sauce, oyster sauce, lemon juice, sugar and mushrooms.

Before serving, garnish with chopped green onion and cilantro.

For a spicier soup, add chile powder or chopped Thai chiles.

ROASTED BUTTERNUT SQUASH SOUP

The Asylum, Jerome

[serves six]

2 large whole butternut squashes, steam roasted

2 poblano peppers, roasted and peeled

2 Anaheim chiles, roasted and peeled

1 white onion, chopped

¾ cup amber beer

2 cups chicken stock

½ cup brown sugar

1 tablespoon garlic, minced

Pinch of cinnamon

Pinch of nutmeg

1 serrano chile, finely minced

1 cup heavy cream

Salt and pepper to taste

Preheat oven to 400 degrees.

Cut the squashes in half and remove the seeds. Place in shallow roasting pans with water and roast until very tender, approximately 45 minutes. Remove from oven and cool.

Roast, peel and de-seed the poblano and Anaheim chiles. Heat skillet until scorching hot. Sauté onions and chiles, then deglaze with beer. Add chicken stock, peeled squash and remaining ingredients, except for the cream. Simmer together for 30 minutes, then purée. Remove from heat and slowly fold in the heavy cream. Add salt and pepper to taste.

BISTRO SALAD

Maynards Market and Kitchen, Tucson

[makes one salad]

¼ cup high-quality applewood bacon slab, uncooked

¼ cup bacon fat

10 bread croutons (use brioche or any loaf bread)

1 soft-boiled egg (method follows)

Whole milk for dredging

Pulverized panko breadcrumbs for dredging

¼ cup baby kale, washed and dried

¼ cup frisée lettuce, washed and dried

½ ounce red onion, julienned

1 tablespoon fine herbs (chopped tarragon, flat-leaf parsley, chives, chervil)

2 tablespoons herb vinaigrette (recipe follows)

Salt and pepper to taste

Preheat oven to 300 degrees.

Slice the bacon into ½-inch strips. Invert the strips and cut half-inch pieces. Place the bacon fat into a heavy-duty saucepan and warm until melted. Add the bacon, bring to a simmer and turn down the heat right before it is fully sizzling. The bacon fat helps keep the lardons from sticking. Continue cooking until the bacon is dark in appearance and slightly chewy, but very tender.

Reserve the bacon fat to fry the croutons in. Cut the bread into 1-inch squares, toss in bacon fat and bake until lightly golden but dry throughout. Reserve for later; reduce oven temperature to 200 degrees.

For the soft egg, add enough cold water in a small saucepan to cover the egg by a half-inch. Bring the water to a boil, then reduce heat to a simmer. Cook the egg for 3 minutes. Immediately place the egg in an ice bath and cool. Carefully peel the egg and reserve.

Warm the bacon in a small pan in the oven. Dredge the egg in milk and panko, fully coating it. Fry the egg until golden brown and drain on a paper towel.

Combine the kale, frisée, onion, herbs, croutons and dressing in a salad bowl and toss well. Add salt and pepper as desired. Neatly arrange the salad on a plate or bowl, and top with the croutons and warm lardons. Carefully cut the egg in half with a bread knife, sprinkle with sea salt, add to salad and serve.

MAYNARDS HERB VINAIGRETTE

2 tablespoons Dijon mustard	2 tablespoons fine herbs (chopped tarragon, flat-leaf parsley, chives, chervil)
¼ cup red wine vinegar	
¾ cup canola oil	Fresh cracked pepper to taste

Preheat oven to 300 degrees.

Whisk together the mustard and vinegar in a bowl. While whisking, slowly pour the oil in a light stream to emulsify. Whisk in the herbs. Refrigerate for up to 4 days. For best results, allow 1 to 2 hours for the herbs to develop.

THAI LETTUCE WRAPS

Blue Buddha Sushi Lounge, Page

[serves four to six]

1 cup mayonnaise
2 tablespoons peach preserves
½ teaspoon salt
½ teaspoon white pepper
2 tablespoons yellow curry powder
¼ cup cilantro, chopped
¼ cup mint, chopped
¼ cup scallions, chopped
2 cloves garlic, finely chopped
4 chicken breasts, cooked and finely chopped
1 head butter lettuce

GARNISH
½ cup carrots, julienned
½ cup pickled beets, julienned
½ cup rice noodles, cooked
½ cup kaiware sprouts

Combine mayonnaise, peach preserves, salt, white pepper, curry powder, cilantro, mint, scallions and garlic, then add the chicken.

Place a large spoonful of the Thai chicken salad on one leaf of butter lettuce, then add the desired garnish.

Serve with sweet chile or hoisin sauce.

HONEYDEW CUCUMBER GAZPACHO

Garland's Oak Creek Lodge, Sedona

[makes 12 12-ounce servings]

¼ loaf rustic white or French bread, crust
    removed, cubed

Vegetable stock

2 English cucumbers

½ honeydew melon, peeled and seeded

¼ bunch celery, rinsed, leaves removed

¼ bunch green onions

1 clove garlic

½ bunch Italian parsley

½ cup basil leaves, chopped

½ cup mint leaves, chopped

1-inch knob of ginger, peeled

2 or 3 limes, juiced

2 teaspoons kosher salt (or to taste)

1 or 2 dashes of Crystal or your preferred hot sauce

Freshly ground black pepper to taste

RESERVE

¼ yellow bell pepper, diced

¼ red bell pepper, diced

Fresh mint sprigs or basil crema
    for garnish

Soak the bread cubes in vegetable stock for 10 to 15 minutes.

Roughly chop the cucumbers, melon, celery, onions, garlic, herbs and ginger, mixing all in a large bowl. Add the lime juice, salt, hot sauce and freshly ground black pepper. Blend in batches until smooth. Strain each batch into another glass or stainless-steel container.

Check the flavor of the soup. Add more lime juice, hot sauce, black pepper and salt as needed.

Chill in your freezer, stirring occasionally. When the soup is thoroughly chilled, cover and store in the refrigerator until ready to serve.

Just before serving, toss the bell peppers into the soup and ladle into bowls.

Garnish the soup with a fresh mint sprig or basil crema.

ENTRÉES

BRAISED BEEF SHORT RIBS

Stables Ranch Grille, Tubac

[serves six]

6 boneless short ribs (about 5 + ¾ pounds)

Kosher salt

Extra-virgin olive oil

1 large Spanish onion, cut into ½-inch pieces

2 ribs celery, cut into ½-inch pieces

2 carrots, peeled, cut in half lengthwise, then cut into ½-inch pieces

2 cloves garlic, smashed

1 + ½ cups tomato paste

2 to 3 cups hearty red wine

2 cups water

1 bunch fresh thyme, tied with kitchen string

2 bay leaves

Season each short rib generously with salt. Coat a pot large enough to accommodate all the meat and vegetables with olive oil and bring to high heat. Add the short ribs to the pan and brown very well, about 2 to 3 minutes per side. Do not overcrowd pan. Cook in batches, if necessary.

Preheat the oven to 375 degrees.

While the short ribs are browning, purée all the vegetables and garlic in a food processor until they form a coarse paste. When the short ribs are very brown on all sides, remove them from the pan. Drain the fat, then coat the bottom of the same pan with fresh oil and add the puréed vegetables. Season the vegetables generously with salt and brown until they are very dark and a crust has formed on the bottom of the pan, approximately 5 to 7 minutes. Scrape the crust and let it re-form. Scrape the crust again and add the tomato paste. Brown the tomato paste for 4 to 5 minutes. Add the wine and scrape the bottom of the pan. Lower the heat if things start to burn. Reduce the mixture by half.

Return the short ribs to the pan and add 2 cups water (or just enough to almost cover the meat). Add the thyme bundle and bay leaves. Cover the pan and place in the preheated oven for 3 hours. Check periodically during the cooking process and add more water if needed. Turn the ribs over halfway through the cooking time. Remove the lid during the last 20 minutes of cooking to let the ribs brown and to let the sauce reduce. When done, the meat should be very tender but not falling apart. Serve with the braising liquid, roasted yams, poblano chiles and caramelized onions.

CHICKEN TERIYAKI PHAT BOWL

Blue Buddha Sushi Lounge, Page

[makes one bowl]

2 tablespoons butter
¼ cup broccoli florets
¼ cup yellow squash, sliced
¼ cup green zucchini, sliced
¼ cup baby corn
¼ cup bok choy, sliced
¼ cup yellow onions, diced
¼ cup mushrooms, thinly sliced
Pinch of salt
Pinch of white pepper
1 chicken breast
½ cup teriyaki sauce
2 cups white rice or udon noodles, cooked

Melt 1 tablespoon of butter in a saucepan. Add all vegetable ingredients, along with salt and white pepper. Sauté until desired tenderness. Set aside and keep warm.

Sauté chicken in 1 tablespoon butter and cook until tender, then add your favorite teriyaki sauce. Toss the chicken in the teriyaki sauce until coated, then cut and slice the chicken.

Add the vegetables and chicken to the rice or noodles. For a moister dish, add additional teriyaki sauce.

HERB-RUBBED ROASTED CHICKEN

Garland's Oak Creek Lodge, Sedona

[serves eight to 10]

4 3 + ½- to 4 + ½-pound chickens
Olive oil
Herb rub (recipe follows)
Lemon-herb vinaigrette (recipe follows)

The night prior to roasting, rinse the chickens inside and out and pat dry. Brush with very little olive oil, then lightly dust the birds inside and out with the rub. Cover and save extra rub for the following day. Refrigerate the chicken overnight, uncovered.

To roast, preheat the oven to 425 degrees. Take the chickens from the fridge and give them another all-over dusting of rub. Tuck the wing tips under and tie the legs together with kitchen string. Arrange in an oiled roasting pan with the legs pointing inward, toward the center of the pan. Roast for 25 minutes, then reduce the temperature to 350 degrees and roast for an additional 35 to 45 minutes, until a lovely, crispy golden brown. The chickens are done when the drumsticks move freely in their sockets.

Remove the meat from the oven and set it aside for 15 minutes. Carve the drumsticks, breasts and wings off the bodies of the birds. Serve a drumstick and thigh or a breast and wing per person with warm lemon-herb vinaigrette.

HERB RUB
2 tablespoons thyme
2 tablespoons sage
2 tablespoons marjoram
2 tablespoons rosemary
Zest of 1 orange
Zest of 1 lemon
¾ cup kosher salt
¼ cup coarse pepper

Lightly toast the dry herbs and zests in a small skillet over medium-low heat. Partially grind the herb/zest mixture in a spice mill and mix with the salt and pepper.

LEMON-HERB VINAIGRETTE

1 + ½ cups lightly packed fresh Italian parsley, basil, mint and/or fennel
4 cloves garlic, minced
2 green onions, finely chopped
2 cups olive oil
½ cup chicken broth
¼ to ⅓ cup lemon juice
1 teaspoon salt
Pepper
Pinch of sugar

Combine the mix of herbs, garlic and green onions in a food processor. Pulse three or four times to blend

slightly. Add one cup of oil and blend. Scrape down the sides of the bowl and blend again.

Add the broth with the machine running, then add the remaining oil slowly. Add lemon juice, 1 teaspoon of salt, a few grinds of fresh pepper and a pinch of

sugar. Blend and taste. Add more lemon juice, salt and pepper if needed. This should be a nice, light emulsion. Transfer to a small double boiler to warm gently.

Makes about 3 to 4 cups. Keeps for two weeks in the refrigerator but loses its bright-green color when heated.

POLLO ALLA RUSTICA

Cucina Rustica, Sedona

[serves four]

4 chicken breasts, lightly pounded
¼ cup flour (for dusting)
½ cup extra-virgin olive oil
Kosher or sea salt
Pepper
½ medium red onion, sliced
1 scant teaspoon garlic, minced
½ cup white wine
½ teaspoon chipotle paste
½ cup marinara sauce
¼ cup cream
½ cup spinach leaves, washed
½ cup chicken broth
¼ cup goat cheese

Begin by dusting both sides of the chicken breasts in flour. Shake off the excess flour and set the chicken aside. Heat a medium skillet over medium-high heat and add oil. When hot, carefully add each chicken breast and season with salt and pepper. Allow the chicken to turn a pale golden-brown before turning. After you turn the meat, add onion slices and continue sautéing until onion is translucent. Add garlic in same fashion and prevent from over-browning by repeatedly turning the breasts until evenly golden.

Deglaze the pan with wine and reduce by half. Add the chipotle paste, marinara and cream, turning to incorporate the sauce. Sprinkle spinach loosely over dish and turn the chicken again to incorporate it. Add the chicken broth, then cover for 2 to 3 minutes until the spinach is wilted. Crumble goat cheese evenly over the dish and cover until serving.

GNOCCARELLI

Enzo's Ristorante Italiano, Snowflake

[serves two]

2 tablespoons olive oil

2 tablespoons red onions, finely diced

3 medium mushrooms, sliced

1 tablespoon red bell peppers, finely diced

8 Kalamata or black olives

2 hot or mild Italian-sausage links, precooked and sliced into ½-inch pieces

Granulated garlic

Pepper

Salt

¼ cup white wine

1 + ½ cups marinara sauce

1 cup shell pasta, cooked

¼ cup Parmesan cheese, grated

⅓ cup mozzarella cheese, shredded

Place olive oil, onions, mushrooms, bell peppers, olives and sausage in a pan and sauté over medium-high heat for 2 minutes. Add a pinch each of granulated garlic, pepper and salt.

Add wine and sauce and bring to a simmer over medium heat. Add the pasta and Parmesan cheese and cook for an additional 2 to 3 minutes. Add mozzarella and stir gently until the cheese is melted, then plate. Use additional cheese or parsley for garnish.

BREADED CATFISH

Twisters 50s Soda Fountain, Williams

[serves six]

1 cup Albers enriched, degermed yellow cornmeal
⅓ cup all-purpose flour
1 tablespoon ground black pepper
1 tablespoon crushed kosher salt
1 tablespoon Lawry's garlic salt
1 teaspoon cayenne pepper
6 6-ounce catfish fillets
Canola oil

For the breading, place the dry ingredients into a large zip-close bag and shake thoroughly.

Slice the catfish into two or three pieces. Tumble the fish in the breading until pieces are completely coated.

Drop the breaded fillets into a 350-degree fryer filled with canola oil.

When the catfish begins to float to the surface of the oil, it's done. The fish should be white and flaky and have a light, golden-brown color.

Serve with lemon wedges, tartar sauce, cocktail sauce or hot sauce.

PECAN-CRUSTED PORK CHOP

Manzanita Restaurant, Cornville

[makes one pork chop]

6-ounce pork loin chop
1 tablespoon cooking oil
2 tablespoons bourbon
2 tablespoons applesauce
2 tablespoons pecans, crumbled
1 tablespoon ginger snaps, ground
2 tablespoons heavy cream
4 tablespoons demi-glace or brown gravy

Preheat oven to 450 degrees.

Pat dry the pork chop with a paper towel. Add oil to a sauté pan and heat on high. When oil just begins to smoke, place the chop into the pan (place one end of chop in the pan closest to you, laying far end last to prevent splattering hot oil). Heat until chop is seared, about 30 to 60 seconds. Drain any remaining oil from the pan and flip the chop, placing the other side down. Remove the pan from the heat, add bourbon and return the pan to the heat.

Carefully light the bourbon so the liquor flames. When the flame goes out, turn off the burner. Spread applesauce on top of the chop, then sprinkle pecan crumbles and ground ginger snaps over the top of the meat.

Add the cream and demi-glace (or brown gravy) to the pan (being careful to avoid getting any on top of the chop). Place the pan in the oven for 7 minutes to finish (or broil chop to finish).

Carefully remove the chop from the pan with a spatula. Pour a little of the sauce on the serving plate, then put the chop on top of the sauce. Pour remaining sauce into a serving ramekin.

ARIZONA TAMALES

Tucson Tamale Co., Tucson

[makes 40 tamales]

FILLING
5 pounds stew or tamale beef, cubed
1 + ¼ cups canned chipotles in adobo
3 cups water
2 14 + ½-ounce cans diced tomatoes

MASA
1 pound butter, margarine or frozen vegetable oil
5 pounds fresh masa dough, unprepared
2 to 3 cups vegetable stock
2 tablespoons baking powder
2 tablespoons (or less) sea salt
4 pounds large corn husks

Put the beef, chipotles, water and one can of tomatoes into a large stock pot. Slowly simmer for 3 hours. Keep an eye on the pot and stir often. If it looks too dry, add a small amount of water. After the meat is fully cooked, add the other can of tomatoes. Using a potato masher, smash the meat to a coarse blend. Put the finished meat into the refrigerator and chill to 40 degrees.

Place the butter, margarine or oil into a bowl and whip until fluffy, about 2 minutes. Beat in the fresh masa alternately with the stock and add the baking powder and salt. Beat until well mixed, then turn the mixer to medium and beat for an additional 10 minutes, or until the masa has the consistency of a thick pancake batter. Put the masa in the refrigerator and cool to 40 degrees.

Soak the corn husks in water for 60 minutes before rolling.

Put a husk in the palm of your hand and evenly spread ½ cup (an ice-cream scoop is a good tool for this step) of masa across the middle of the husk with a spatula or the back of a large spoon. In the center of the masa, place ½ cup of the beef mix. Fold both sides of the husk, one over the other, over the filling. Add a second corn husk and place the tamale so the exposed top is now enclosed.

Place all the tamales into a large steamer pot with a steamer basket with 3 to 4 inches of hot water on the bottom. Layer the tamales in a crisscross pattern. Bring to a high boil and start timing the steaming process when the steam is rising out of the pot. Cover the tamales with leftover corn husks or a clean, damp kitchen towel, then cover the pot. Reduce the heat to medium-high and steam for 35 minutes. Take the tamales out of the pot and let them sit for 10 minutes before eating.

CHILE RELLENO

Santiago's, Bisbee

[serves four to six]

12 Anaheim green chiles
1 + ½ cups Oaxaca cheese
6 egg whites
1 egg yolk
2 tablespoons all-purpose flour
Oil for frying
Tomatillo sauce and ancho spread for garnish

Fire-roast or fry chiles until skin pops and changes color. Hold in a container covered with plastic wrap for 10 minutes, allowing chiles to steam and to help separate the skin from the chiles.

Remove skin and make a small slit to remove seeds, leaving stem intact. Stuff chiles with a 2-inch-long, half-inch-wide stick of Oaxaca cheese. Use caution to not overstuff or tear chiles.

In a frozen stainless-steel bowl, whip the egg whites until they form stiff peaks, approximately 3 to 5 minutes. Add the egg yolk and flour and mix for an additional minute.

Heat 2 inches of oil to 375 degrees.

Dust peppers lightly in flour before dipping in batter and then into the oil to fry until golden brown.

To plate, top with tomatillo sauce and garnish with ancho spread.

SHRIMP SCAMPI

Gerardo's Firewood Café, Payson

[serves two]

2 tablespoons olive oil

2 tablespoons herb butter

16 shrimp, cleaned and peeled

1 tablespoon lemon oil

1 teaspoon garlic, chopped

1 teaspoon lemon zest

½ cup white wine

1 + ¼ cups (10 ounces) linguine pasta

Salt and pepper to taste

2 tablespoons Italian parsley, coarsely chopped

Heat olive oil in a sauté pan. Add 1 tablespoon herb butter, then add shrimp and sauté. When the shrimp is half-cooked, add lemon oil, chopped garlic, lemon zest and white wine.

Meanwhile, boil the linguine pasta al dente, then strain and add to sauté pan with shrimp. Add 1 tablespoon herb butter, lemon oil, salt, pepper and Italian parsley.

FLAT IRON STEAK WITH DR PEPPER MARINADE

Liberty Market, Gilbert

[serves four]

2 cups Dr Pepper
⅛ cup Worcestershire sauce
⅛ cup olive oil
½ tablespoon chopped garlic
1 teaspoon salt
1 teaspoon pepper
4 flat iron steaks

Whisk together Dr Pepper, Worcestershire sauce, olive oil, garlic, salt and pepper. Pour the marinade over the steaks, cover and refrigerate for 24 hours.

Remove the steaks from the marinade and grill to taste.

SMOKED CHICKEN ENCHILADAS

Elote Café, Sedona

[serves four]

Olive oil as needed
½ cup chopped onions
3 cloves garlic, peeled and roughly chopped
1 poblano chile, roughly chopped
1 jalapeño, chopped
4 cups tomatillos, husked, rinsed and chopped
2 cups chicken stock
½ cup chopped cilantro
8 thick corn tortillas
4 cups smoked chicken, pulled or shredded
2 cups jack cheese, shredded

Preheat oven to 375 degrees.

In a saucepan over medium-high heat, cook the onions, garlic, poblano and jalapeño until lightly browned, then add the remaining ingredients, except cilantro. Simmer until soft. Purée with cilantro and reserve.

Warm tortillas in a large dry skillet and dip into the sauce. Fill each one with about ½ cup of chicken and a tablespoon or so of cheese. Roll the tortillas and place them in a greased baking dish. Pour the remaining sauce over the top and sprinkle with the remaining cheese. Bake for 10 minutes.

MOLLY'S SPECIAL STEAK AND MORMON GRAVY

Molly Butler Lodge, Greer

[makes one steak]

½ pound butter

½ pound ground beef

1 + ½ cups flour

2 teaspoons pepper

2 teaspoons ham base

2 teaspoons seasoned salt

1 can evaporated milk

4 to 6 cups water

1 certified Angus beef sirloin, sliced into ½-inch medallions and seasoned with Montreal steak seasoning

Melt butter in a saucepan and brown beef on medium heat. Add the flour, pepper, ham base and seasoned salt. Reduce heat to low and continue cooking roux for 5 to 10 minutes. Add evaporated milk and 4 cups water, and boil until gravy thickens. If the gravy becomes too thick, add 2 more cups water until the sauce is to your liking.

Grill the steak to taste, then smother with gravy.

NEW ZEALAND RACK OF LAMB

Cliff Dwellers Restaurant, Vermilion Cliffs

[serves four]

8-bone lamb rack
½ cup Dijon mustard
3 cloves garlic, finely chopped
1 tablespoon fresh thyme
Salt and pepper to taste
¼ cup panko breadcrumbs

Preheat oven to 350 degrees.

Take a clean and trimmed rack of lamb and season with salt and pepper. Sear all exposed meat in a hot sauté pan with a little oil, making sure not to cook the meat. Set aside to cool.

Mix mustard, garlic, thyme, salt and pepper. Once the meat is cooled, spread the mixture over the exposed meat and coat with the breadcrumbs. Sear the meat again to brown the breadcrumbs. Bake for about 15 minutes to serve at medium rare. Let rest for 5 minutes before serving.

EL TOVAR NAVAJO TACO

El Tovar Dining Room, Grand Canyon National Park

[serves four]

FRY BREAD

1 + ½ cups plus 2 tablespoons all-purpose flour

½ cup nonfat dry milk powder

1 + ½ teaspoons baking powder

¼ teaspoon salt

2 tablespoons plus 1 + ½ teaspoons Crisco, chilled and cut into small pieces

½ cup ice water

1 cup Crisco for frying

MEAT

½ pound ground beef

1 teaspoon chili powder

1 teaspoon ground cumin

1 pinch cayenne pepper

½ teaspoon granulated garlic

½ teaspoon granulated onion

Pinch of salt

¼ cup hot sauce

1 can black beans, drained and rinsed

1 can kidney beans, drained and rinsed

FRY BREAD

In a large bowl, mix flour, nonfat dry milk, baking powder and salt. Cut in Crisco until it resembles fine crumbs. Add the ice water and mix the dough until it pulls cleanly away from sides of bowl.

Cover with a towel and set aside for 2 hours.

Divide the dough into four equal pieces and shape each into a circle by hand. Roll each piece on a floured cutting board to ¼-inch thick. Poke your finger through center of each to make a hole.

Heat 1 cup of Crisco in a large cast-iron skillet over medium-high heat. When fat is hot, add 1 piece of dough and fry for 3 to 4 minutes per side. Remove the bread from the skillet and allow to drain on a plate lined with paper towels. Cover to keep warm while you repeat process with remaining dough.

MEAT

Heat a medium-size heavy skillet over medium-high heat. Add beef and cook until browned. Drain excess fat.

Add remaining ingredients and bring to a boil.

Divide topping evenly among 4 pieces of fry bread. Top as desired with shredded lettuce, diced tomato and shredded cheddar cheese. Serve with sides of sour cream and your favorite salsa.

CRISPY PORK CARNITAS

The Turquoise Room at La Posada, Winslow

[serves four]

1 cup granulated garlic
¼ cup ground cumin
¼ cup kosher salt
½ cup ground black pepper
1 quart corn oil
3 pounds boneless pork shoulder, cut into 4-inch pieces
1 orange, quartered with skin on

Mix together garlic, cumin, salt and pepper and place into a shallow bowl.

Place the oil into a large, high-sided stock pot and heat it to 300 degrees. Roll the meat pieces in the seasoning mix and place them carefully into the oil. Turn the heat to low so the oil simmers. Add the orange quarters to the oil. Cook for 1 + ½ to 2 hours, or until the meat is tender, but not falling apart. If the pork begins to blacken, reduce the heat.

After cooking, remove the pork with a slotted spoon and place on a baker's rack to drain. Discard the orange pieces.

When the meat has cooled, remove any excess pieces of grease. (At this point, the meat may be wrapped tightly, placed in a freezer bag and stored in the refrigerator until needed. The meat can be prepared up to three days ahead of making the carnitas.)

If you have cooked the pork in advance, reheat it by placing it on a baking sheet under the oven broiler on low. Heat it for 15 to 20 minutes, depending on how hot the broiler is, turning at least once during the reheating process. It should be sizzling, crispy and a golden-brown color.

Serve with basic black beans, red-chile sauce and papaya salsa (see recipes, page 124).

Spoon the beans into the center of a plate and place the pork on top. Ladle a thread of the red-chile sauce around the beans. Top the meat with a couple of tablespoons of the papaya salsa, letting the juices from the salsa run down over the meat.

ENTRÉES

BLUTARSKY BURGER

Diablo Burger, Flagstaff

[makes one burger]

6 ounces ground beef
Cajun seasoning
Sharp cheddar cheese, sliced
Bacon slices, cooked
Guacamole (recipe follows)
English muffin, toasted

GUACAMOLE
3 limes
12 avocados, halved and pitted
⅛ cup garlic, roasted
2 tomatoes, diced
½ red onion, diced
1 + ½ jalapeños, diced
½ bunch cilantro, roughly chopped
Salt and pepper to taste

For the guacamole, juice the limes on top of the avocados and add the roasted garlic. Mash the avocados with the lime juice and garlic until a smooth consistency has been achieved. Stir in the diced vegetables and cilantro until fully incorporated. Liberally season with salt and pepper.

Loosely form a beef patty 4 inches wide and 1 inch thick, and season to taste with salt and pepper. Cook to desired temperature, and try to turn the patty only once to avoid losing any of the juices. Dust with Cajun seasoning. Top with a thick slice of sharp cheddar and 2 slices of bacon.

Spread a thick layer of guacamole on the top bun and place burger on the bottom bun.

CAVATELLI WITH SAUSAGE

Brix, Flagstaff

[serves four]

2 cups flour
1 tablespoon kosher salt
1 egg
¼ cup water
¼ cup + 1 tablespoon extra-virgin olive oil
2 tablespoons red-chile flakes
2 tablespoons extra-virgin olive oil (for sautéing)
¼ pound ground Italian sausage
1 cup oyster mushrooms, sliced
1 bunch broccoli rabe, chopped
3 tablespoons Marcona almonds, chopped
Parmesan cheese, grated

In a mixing bowl, combine the flour and salt. In separate bowl, lightly whisk together egg, water and 1 tablespoon olive oil. Run mixer on low speed, and gradually add water until dough forms.

Once dough forms, turn out on floured cutting board and knead for 10 minutes. When dough is kneaded, wrap in plastic wrap and let rest for a minimum of 30 minutes.

Once rested, roll dough out to ¼-inch thick. (Sprinkle all-purpose flour on surface to prevent sticking.) Cut dough into ½-inch strips, then cut strips into 3-inch rectangles. Using three fingers, press and roll pasta rectangles toward you. This will create three cups in each pasta piece. Flour a plate to store pasta for later use.

In a blender, add chile flakes and ¼ cup oil. Blend until chile flakes are combined with oil and oil is red in color. Reserve chile oil in a small kitchen bowl.

In a large saucepan, add water and a pinch of salt for blanching pasta.

In large sauté pan over medium-high heat, add olive oil and ground sausage. Break up the sausage with the back of a kitchen spoon. Cook through, then add mushrooms, broccoli rabe and almonds. Sauté for 6 minutes on low heat.

At this time, begin cooking the pasta. Boil for 6 to 10 minutes (pasta will float to the top of the water when cooked).

Add pasta to sausage mixture with 3 tablespoons of pasta water to create sauce. Add 1 tablespoon of chile oil and toss. Finish with desired amount of chile oil and Parmesan.

RIGATONI CON SALSICCIA E FUNGHI

Caffe Torino Ristorante Italiano, Oro Valley

[serves four]

1 pound rigatoni
2 tablespoons extra-virgin olive oil
4 sweet Italian sausages, casing removed
2 red bell peppers, sliced
1 pound white mushrooms, sliced
4 cloves garlic, chopped
¼ cup dry porcini mushrooms, softened in water and chopped
¼ cup dry white wine
2 cups tomato sauce
Splash of heavy cream
Salt and pepper to taste

Cook the rigatoni in salted boiling water.

In a heavy saucepan, heat the oil. Break the sausage into pieces and cook it over medium heat. Add the bell peppers and mushrooms and let cook until the sausage is cooked through and the vegetables are softened. Add the garlic and porcini mushrooms and cook for 2 additional minutes.

Deglaze the mixture with white wine. When the wine evaporates, add the tomato sauce and a splash of heavy cream. Add salt and pepper to taste. Let simmer for about 5 minutes. Drain the pasta and add the sauce. Garnish with Parmigiano Reggiano cheese.

SRIRACHA TUNA SANDWICH ON ROSEMARY FOCACCIA

Josephine's, Flagstaff

[serves two]

1 fresh ahi tuna steak, seared rare (or to preference)
  and sliced
Rosemary focaccia (recipe follows)
Sriracha aioli (recipe follows)
Radish sprouts
Fresh tomatoes, sliced
Jicama, julienned

ROSEMARY FOCACCIA
3 cups warm water (not hot)
1 tablespoon yeast
¼ cup olive oil
8 cups bread flour
2 tablespoons salt
1 tablespoon garlic, minced
½ cup Parmesan cheese, grated
Salt and pepper
2 tablespoons fresh rosemary, finely chopped

SRIRACHA AIOLI
8 cloves garlic, roasted in olive oil and minced
1 teaspoon kosher or sea salt
Juice of 2 lemons
½ cup Egg Beaters
¼ cup sesame oil
2 tablespoons honey
1 cup Sriracha
1 cup canola oil
1 cup extra-virgin olive oil

For the focaccia, place water, yeast and ¼ cup olive oil in a mixing bowl and allow to ferment.

Add the flour and salt and knead in mixer for 12 minutes with a dough hook. Let rest overnight in refrigerator. Take out of refrigerator, cover with a damp cloth and set in a warm place until the dough doubles in size.

For the Sriracha aioli, combine all ingredients except the canola oil and extra-virgin olive oil in a plastic container. Using an immersion blender, slowly add the canola oil, then the olive oil. If needed, add water to thin the sauce.

Preheat oven to 375 degrees.

Grease and flour a sheet pan. Roll out focaccia dough on sheet pan. Spread remaining ¼ cup olive oil, garlic, Parmesan, salt and pepper atop the focaccia. Sprinkle with chopped rosemary. Let the focaccia proof once more in a warm place, then bake for 12 minutes, rotating once.

To assemble the sandwich, spread slices of rosemary focaccia bread with Sriracha aioli, arrange tuna slices on top, and serve with radish sprouts, sliced tomato and jicama.

CHILES EN NOGADA

Barrio Café, Phoenix

[serves four]

2 + ½ tablespoons vegetable oil
2 skinless, boneless chicken breasts, diced
2 teaspoons onions, diced
1 teaspoon apples, diced
1 teaspoon dried apricots, diced
1 teaspoon dried cranberries
1 teaspoon pears, diced
1 teaspoon raisins
2 cloves garlic, minced
2 teaspoons tomato paste
1 cup dry white wine
Sugar
Salt and freshly ground pepper
4 poblano peppers, roasted and peeled
1 shallot, minced
1 cup dry white wine
2 cups heavy cream
¼ cup almonds, ground
1 teaspoon fresh cilantro leaves (for garnish)
1 teaspoon pomegranate seeds (for garnish)

In a medium sauté pan, heat 1 tablespoon vegetable oil over medium heat. Add the chicken and cook until it starts to turn white, about 5 minutes. Add the onions and cook until translucent, about 5 minutes. Add the apples, apricots, cranberries, pears, raisins and half the garlic, and cook for 2 minutes. Stir in the tomato paste and cook for 2 more minutes. Add the wine and simmer until the chicken is tender, about 5 minutes. Season with sugar, salt and pepper, then remove from the heat.

Stuff each roasted poblano pepper with one-quarter of the chicken mixture and set aside.

In a medium sauté pan over medium-low heat, cook the shallots in 1 + ½ tablespoons vegetable oil until translucent, about 3 minutes. Add the remaining garlic and cook until it turns a light caramel color, about 5 minutes. Add the wine and simmer until it is almost completely evaporated, about 15 minutes. Add the heavy cream and simmer until reduced by half, about 15 more minutes. Stir in the almonds and season with salt and pepper.

To serve, place each stuffed poblano pepper on a plate and top with 2 tablespoons sauce. Garnish with the cilantro and pomegranate seeds.

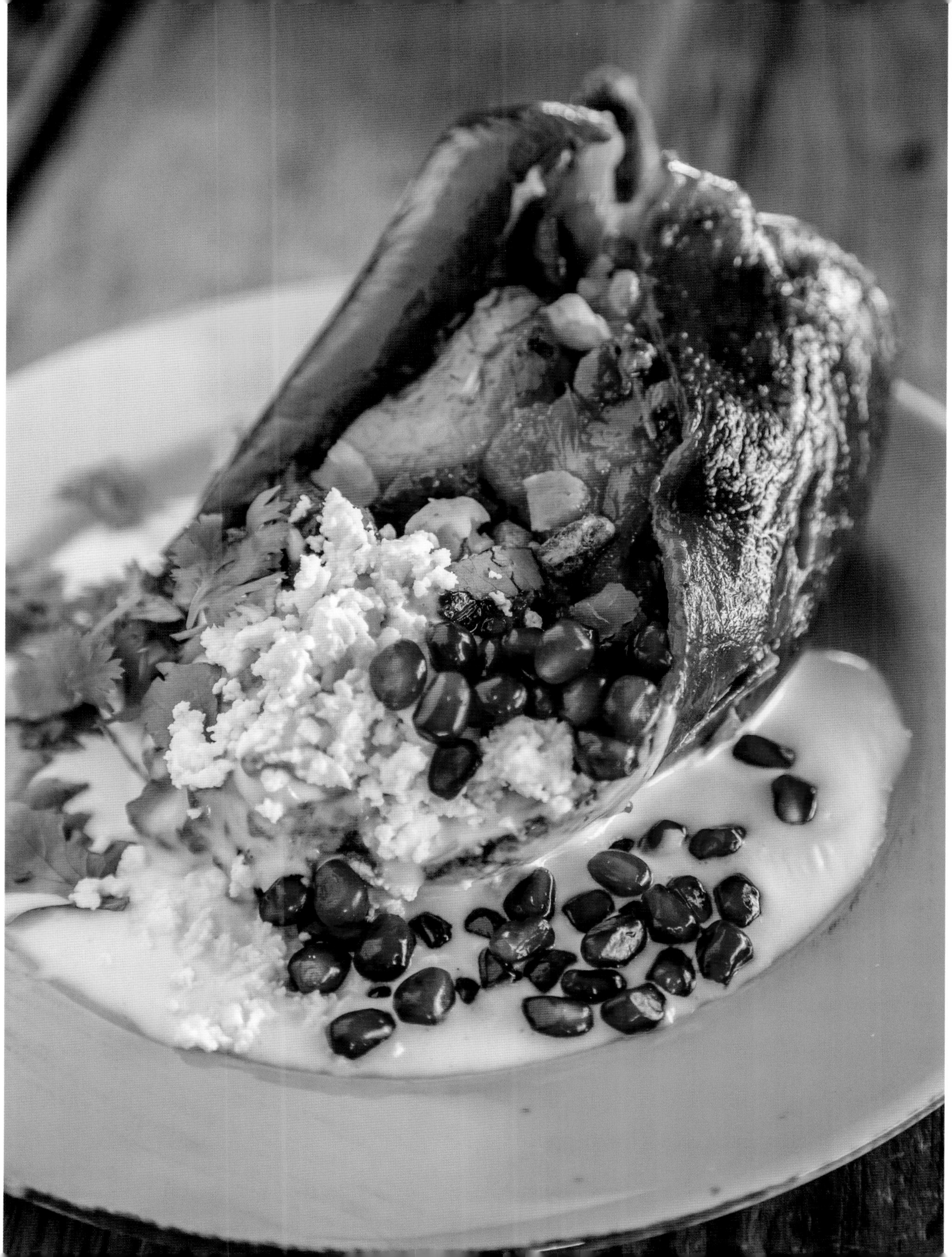

SCREAMING BANSHEE PIZZA

Screaming Banshee, Bisbee

[serves two]

All-purpose flour (for dusting)
8-ounce ball pizza dough, thawed if frozen
Extra-virgin olive oil (for drizzling)
¼ cup mushrooms, roasted
¼ cup sweet onions, caramelized
8 ounces fresh mozzarella cheese
½ cup fennel sausage
Fresh parsley, chopped

Put a pizza stone in the oven and preheat the oven to 500 degrees, allowing at least 30 minutes for the stone to heat.

On a floured surface, roll or stretch the dough out to a 12-inch round. Transfer the dough to a floured pizza peel. Lightly drizzle olive oil over the dough. Evenly add the roasted mushrooms, roasted onions and fresh mozzarella on top of the dough. Place sausage on top of the cheese.

Slide the pizza onto the stone and bake for about 4 minutes, until lightly golden and bubbling. Carefully spin the pizza on the stone and bake for 2 minutes longer, until the crust is browned. Slide the pizza onto a work surface and sprinkle the parsley over the top. Cut into wedges and serve.

LILA'S SPECIAL TOSTADA

Wisdom's Café, Tumacacori

[servings vary]

Pinto beans, slow-cooked with half an onion, salt,
  pepper and vegetable oil
Iceberg lettuce, shredded
Shredded beef or turkey (slow-cook boneless meat of
  your choice in water with half an onion, salt, pepper
  and a clove of garlic, then drain and shred)
Cheddar-jack cheese, shredded
Avocado, sliced
Tomato, sliced
Corn tostada shells

Layer the turkey or beef, beans, lettuce, cheese, tomato
and avocado slices atop the corn tostadas.

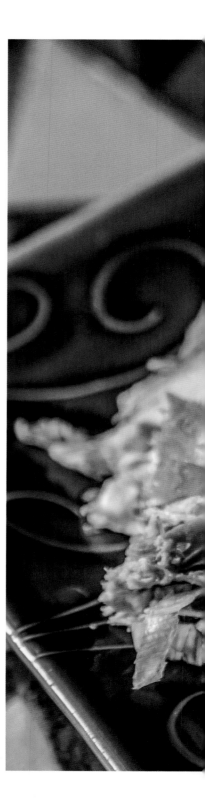

PAN-SEARED AIRLINE BREAST OF CHICKEN WITH FINGERLING POTATO HASH

Rancho de los Caballeros, Wickenburg

[serves four]

4 chicken-breast halves
8 purple, red or fingerling potatoes (golf-ball sized)
Oil
Salt and pepper to taste
1 cup corn niblets
½ cup red and green bell peppers, julienned

Have your grocery butcher remove the wing portion of the chicken, leaving the drumette intact. Have the butcher remove the breast from the body, leaving the skin and drumette attached.

Preheat oven to 375 degrees.

Wash potatoes thoroughly, then pat dry with a paper towel. Cut potatoes in half, then place into a bowl. Add oil, season with salt and pepper, and toss to coat potatoes. Layer potatoes in a baking pan and bake for 30 to 35 minutes, or until cooked. Remove from oven and set aside.

Reduce oven temperature to 350 degrees, then preheat an oven-proof sauté pan large enough to hold the chicken. Season the chicken breasts on both sides with salt and pepper. Pour 1 tablespoon of oil into the preheated sauté pan, then sear the chicken, skin side down, for 3 or 4 minutes. Turn the chicken over and sear the other side for another 3 or 4 minutes. Place chicken in preheated oven for 20 to 25 minutes.

Preheat another sauté pan. Add 1 teaspoon of oil, then add corn and stir for 1 minute. Add potatoes and stir, then add bell peppers and salt and pepper to taste. Set aside and keep warm.

Check chicken for doneness. The thickest part of the breast should be 165 degrees.

Divide the corn, bell peppers and potatoes onto four plates, and place chicken breasts on top. Spoon pan drippings from chicken-roasting pan over chicken breasts. Serve immediately.

ARTICHOKE AND PORTOBELLO MUSHROOM LASAGNA

Cafe Roka, Bisbee

[serves eight to 10]

2 tablespoons olive oil

1 large onion, diced into medium-sized pieces

4 garlic cloves, minced

1 pound portobello mushrooms, diced into medium-
sized pieces

14-ounce can artichokes (in water), drained and
coarsely chopped

1 pound fresh, cleaned spinach, roughly cut

Salt and pepper to taste

4 tablespoons butter

4 tablespoons flour

4 + ½ cups milk

14-ounce can diced tomatoes, drained

1 + ½ cups Parmesan, grated

Nutmeg to taste

1 box oven-ready, no-boil lasagna sheets

1 pound whole-milk mozzarella, thinly sliced

In large skillet over high heat, add the olive oil and onions and cook for 2 minutes. Add the garlic and mushrooms and cook an additional 3 or 4 minutes until the mushrooms release moisture. Add drained, coarsely chopped artichokes, and continue cooking for 2 or 3 minutes. Transfer to large mixing bowl. Add fresh spinach to warm mixture in bowl, then toss to wilt. Season with salt and pepper, then set aside.

Melt butter in medium saucepan over medium-high heat until foamy. Stir in the flour and cook for 1 minute, continuing to stir. Slowly whisk in the milk and drained tomatoes. Lower heat to medium-low and continue cooking, stirring constantly for 7 or 8 minutes until the sauce is thick enough to coat the back of the spoon. Stir in the Parmesan cheese and season to taste with salt, pepper and nutmeg.

Preheat oven to 350 degrees.

To assemble the lasagna, ladle ¾ cup of tomato-bechamel sauce into the bottom of a 9-by-13-inch pan and spread evenly. Cover with lasagna noodles. Spoon one-quarter of the vegetable mixture over noodles. Ladle another ¾ cup of sauce over vegetable mixture. Repeat to four layers. Top with remaining mozzarella. Cover with foil and bake for 45 minutes. Remove foil and increase heat to 450 degrees. Bake an additional 15 minutes to brown top. Let rest 10 minutes before serving.

SHRIMP PAD THAI

Dara Thai Café, Williams

[serves one]

⅓ cup rice noodles
10 shrimp
1 egg
¼ cup water
3 tablespoons fish sauce
2 tablespoons vinegar
2 tablespoons sugar
1 teaspoon paprika
¼ cup bean sprouts
2 tablespoons green onions, chopped
1 tablespoon peanuts, crushed
Chile pepper (optional)

Soak the rice noodles in room-temperature water for approximately 30 minutes.

Heat the wok, add the shrimp and egg, and cook for 2 minutes before adding the noodles and water. Stir-fry until all ingredients are well mixed.

Add the fish sauce, vinegar, sugar and paprika. Stir-fry quickly and add bean sprouts and green onions, ensuring everything is well combined. Garnish with crushed peanuts just prior to serving.

PRICKLY PEAR BARBECUED
PORK TENDERLOIN

The Asylum, Jerome

[serves eight]

½ cup vegetable oil

1 tablespoon achiote paste

Juice of ½ fresh-squeezed orange

2 tablespoons cilantro

1 tablespoon Sonoran Spice or equivalent
(non-hydrolyzed taco seasoning)

½ teaspoon salt and pepper, or to taste

3- to 4-pound pork tenderloin

2 cups barbecue sauce

½ cup prickly pear syrup

Blend vegetable oil, achiote paste and fresh-squeezed orange juice until smooth. Add the cilantro and spices. Pour the marinade over the tenderloin, coat evenly and let chill for 2 to 24 hours.

Combine barbecue sauce and prickly pear syrup.

Grill 7-ounce portions of marinated pork tenderloin per person to medium rare.

Brush with prickly pear barbecue sauce while the pork is on the grill to caramelize sugar in sauce. Let rest for 10 minutes, then cut each 7-ounce portion straight down into four small fillets. Serve over mashed potatoes or with fresh steamed veggies.

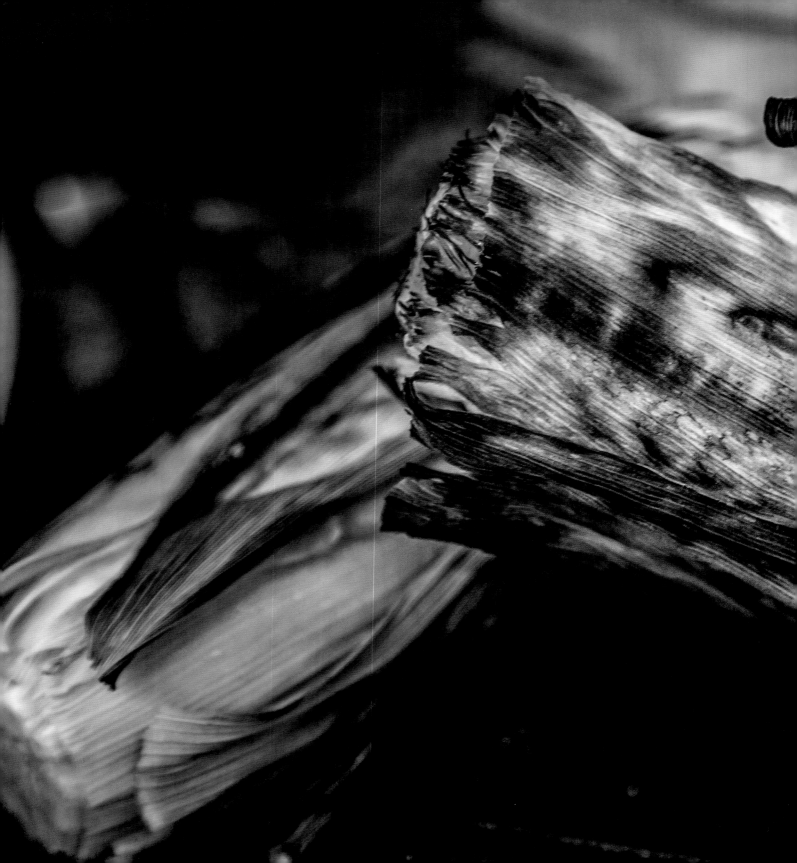

SIDES & SAUCES

VEGETABLE STRUDEL

Manzanita Restaurant, Cornville

[serves 20]

1 cup carrots, finely diced
1 cup celery, finely diced
1 cup yellow onions, finely diced
¾ cup red bell peppers, finely diced
½ cup green bell peppers, finely diced
1 cup zucchini, finely diced
1 cup yellow squash, finely diced
1 teaspoon Italian seasoning
1 teaspoon basil
1 teaspoon salt
1 teaspoon black pepper
1 teaspoon celery salt
1 teaspoon oregano
2 tablespoons butter
20 sheets phyllo dough

Combine vegetables and spices, then sauté in butter until tender, about 5 minutes. Remove from heat.

Separately, melt ½ cup butter in a small saucepan to use for sealing the edges of the wrapped strudels.

Spread a single phyllo-dough sheet on a flat surface and fold it in half lengthwise. Place about ¼ cup of sautéed vegetables near the center of the bottom edge of the phyllo dough. Spread the vegetables over a 1-by-4-inch section, leaving the edges free so they can be folded over to seal the strudel after rolling it. Gently roll the phyllo dough around the vegetables, continuing up the length of the phyllo dough. Brush a small amount of the melted butter along the edges of the dough and fold to seal the strudel. Cook the strudels in a skillet over medium heat. It is not necessary to add oil to the pan, as the butter in the phyllo dough provides enough oil. Cook until the dough is crisp and the vegetable filling is hot.

TODD'S FIRE SALSA

Tucson Tamale Co., Tucson

[makes 3 quarts]

4 ounces jalapeños
1 ounce garlic, peeled
2 26-ounce cans diced tomatoes
½ tablespoon brown sugar
2 tablespoons oregano
1 tablespoon sea salt
1 tablespoon black pepper
4 cups water
3 ounces fresh cilantro
16-ounce can chipotles in adobo

Preheat oven to 375 degrees.

Roast the jalapeños and garlic for 25 minutes. Assemble
all ingredients in a blender and purée for 3 minutes.
Refrigerate and serve.

ELOTE

Elote Café, Sedona

[serves six]

6 ears corn, husks intact
1 cup mayonnaise
1 tablespoon Cholula hot sauce
2 tablespoons fresh lime juice
¼ cup chicken stock
1 teaspoon salt
1 teaspoon pepper
1 teaspoon sugar
¼ cup cotija cheese, ground
2 tablespoons cilantro, chopped
Pure ground chile powder to taste

Over a medium-hot grill, roast the corn until the husks are well charred, about 5 minutes. Turn the husks occasionally so as not to completely burn the kernels underneath. Set them aside to cool, then shuck and cut the corn off the cob. When ready to eat, mix the mayonnaise, hot sauce, lime juice, chicken stock, salt, pepper and sugar, and warm in a sauté pan with the corn. Pour into a bowl and garnish with the cheese, cilantro and chile powder. Serve immediately.

POBLANO BLACK BEAN RICE

El Tovar Dining Room, Grand Canyon National Park

[serves four]

½ ounce cottonseed oil
½ yellow onion, diced into small pieces
¼ cup poblano chiles, roasted and diced
¼ cup canned black beans, drained and rinsed
3 cups cooked white rice
1 tablespoon cilantro, chopped
Salt and pepper to taste
1 cup sour cream
2 tablespoons lime juice

Heat a sauté pan over medium-high heat, add oil and sauté onion until translucent.
Add chiles and beans and cook until hot. Add rice and incorporate until mixed. Add
cilantro, salt and pepper to taste. Whisk together sour cream and lime juice and use
to garnish the beans.

HOPI HUMMUS

The Turquoise Room at La Posada, Winslow

[makes 6 cups]

BEANS

1 cup white tepary beans
½ cup onions, diced
½ cup celery, diced
½ cup carrots, diced
1 tablespoon garlic, chopped
1 teaspoon salt
1 bay leaf
4 cups water

Place ingredients in a saucepan and cook until the beans are soft and tender. Add more water if needed. When cooked, remove the bay leaf and let the beans cool. Refrigerate while the rest of the recipe is prepared.

HUMMUS

2 cups fresh corn, cut off the cob and roasted
2 tablespoons Dijon mustard
1 teaspoon garlic, chopped
1 teaspoon sea salt
½ teaspoon freshly ground pepper
½ cup sunflower seed oil
1 cup corn oil

Put the prepared beans, corn, mustard, garlic, salt and pepper into a food processor and purée. Slowly add the oils until smooth.

The hummus can be stored in a sealed container in the refrigerator for one week.

PEPERONATA

Caffe Torino Ristorante Italiano, Oro Valley

[serves two]

½ cup extra-virgin olive oil
1 medium yellow onion, sliced thin
6 bell peppers (a combination of red and yellow), sliced into 2-inch pieces
4 cloves of garlic, smashed
1 can peeled tomatoes
2 bay leaves
Several leaves fresh basil
Salt and pepper to taste

In a large frying pan, heat the oil and add the onions and bell peppers. Let them cook until softened. Add the smashed garlic and let it cook for a few more minutes. Break the peeled tomatoes with your hand and add them to the pan. Add the bay leaves, fresh basil, salt and pepper to taste. Let it cook on low heat for about 30 minutes until the sauce is reduced and the peppers are cooked. Remove the bay leaves.

Enjoy the blend as a side dish, on top of crostini or as a pasta sauce.

TINDERBOX BLUE-CHEESE GRITS

Tinderbox Kitchen, Flagstaff

[serves four]

3 cups water
4 cups half-and-half
3 tablespoons honey
1 + ½ cups Quaker instant hominy grits
2 cups blue cheese, crumbled
Kosher salt to taste
Cracked black pepper to taste

Bring water, half-and-half and honey to a simmer
slowly. Whisk in grits and turn down heat to low.
Simmer for 40 minutes on low. If too thick, add a
splash of water. Whisk in blue cheese and season with
salt and pepper.

FRIED GREEN TOMATOES

Josephine's, Flagstaff

[serves eight]

1 cup pepitas (pumpkin seeds)
1 cup cornmeal
1 tablespoon salt and pepper
8 green tomatoes, cut into ¼-inch slices
2 cups flour
Egg wash (3 eggs beaten with 1 cup milk)
Butter
Pickled red onions (recipe follows)
Ancho aioli (recipe follows)

In a food processor, chop up pepitas until they're in small pieces. Mix with cornmeal, salt and pepper to taste.

Coat sliced green tomatoes with flour, tap excess flour off and then coat in egg wash. Finally, coat with cornmeal mixture.

Heat butter in sauté pan until sizzling. Pan-fry tomatoes on each side. Arrange on a plate with pickled red onions in the center. Drizzle a swirl of ancho aioli on top of each tomato.

PICKLED RED ONIONS

1 cup apple-cider vinegar
1 cup water
¼ cup sugar
1 tablespoon salt
3 bay leaves
2 red onions, slivered
1 or 2 serrano chiles, sliced thin

Combine the vinegar, water, sugar, salt and bay leaves and bring to a boil. Add the red onions and chiles and return to a boil. Strain and cool the liquid and onions separately. Once cool, combine and refrigerate.

ANCHO AIOLI

8 cloves garlic, roasted and chopped
1 teaspoon kosher or sea salt
2 limes, juiced
½ cup Egg Beaters
¼ cup ancho chili powder
2 tablespoons honey
1 tablespoon Tabasco sauce
1 cup canola oil
1 cup extra-virgin olive oil

Place the first seven ingredients into a plastic container. Then, using an immersion blender, add the canola oil, then the olive oil. If needed, add water to thin the aioli.

BASIC BLACK BEANS, RED-CHILE SAUCE AND PAPAYA SALSA

The Turquoise Room at La Posada, Winslow

BASIC BLACK BEANS

[makes 4 to 6 cups]

1 pound black beans, washed and soaked for 12 hours
½ tablespoon New Mexico mild chile powder
1 teaspoon ground cumin
½ teaspoon oregano
½ teaspoon marjoram
½ teaspoon ground coriander
½ teaspoon chipotle purée (recipe follows)
¼ teaspoon ground white pepper
1 small bay leaf
½ cup white onion, diced
1 teaspoon salt
4 cloves garlic, chopped
2 tablespoons unsalted butter or olive oil
1 quart water

One day ahead, wash the beans and leave to soak overnight in cold water.

Place all the ingredients in a large, thick-bottomed pot. Bring to a boil and simmer for 1 + ½ hours until the beans are tender, adding water as needed. Depending on how quickly you simmer the beans, the water will evaporate. Remove the bay leaf and discard.

Place a third of the beans in a blender and blend until smooth, diluting with water as needed. Return the blended beans to the main bean mixture. (Blending a third of the beans adds a creamy consistency to the dish. Leaving them unblended tends to make the dish watery and soup-like.)

CHIPOTLE PURÉE
1 can (any size) chipotle in adobado sauce
1 can water

Place the entire contents of a can of chipotle in adobado sauce into a blender. Fill the empty can with water and add the water to the blender. Blend until smooth. The sauce may be kept in the refrigerator in a sealed container for weeks.

RED-CHILE SAUCE [makes 6 cups]

½ cup white onions, sliced
2 cloves garlic, sliced
2 tablespoons olive oil
4 arbol chiles (or 2 arbol chiles and 1 Oaxaca chile)
½ teaspoon ground coriander
½ teaspoon ground cumin

Pour into a blender and process until smooth. Pass through a fine strainer. Cool and store in a sealed container in the refrigerator.

GUAJILLO PURÉE

2 ounces guajillo chile pods (New Mexico chiles may be substituted)

2 cups water

Using food-handler gloves, remove the seeds and stems from the chiles. Place them in a saucepan with the water and simmer for 15 minutes. Pour into a blender and blend until smooth. Pour through a fine strainer to remove any remaining seeds and the skins. Cool and store the purée in a sealed container in the refrigerator. It will keep for one week.

PAPAYA SALSA [makes 4 cups]

2 cups papaya, diced into ¼-inch pieces

1 cup cherry or baby Roma tomatoes, sliced in half

¼ cup red onion, diced

1 or 2 jalapeños, seeded and finely diced

2 tablespoons orange juice

2 tablespoons lime juice (key lime preferable)

2 tablespoons hazelnut oil

2 tablespoons seasoned rice vinegar

½ teaspoon sea salt

⅛ teaspoon white pepper, finely ground

⅛ teaspoon ginger, ground

1 whole orange

Place all the ingredients into a mixing bowl and toss carefully until well coated with the oil and juices. Refrigerate in a sealed container until needed.

½ teaspoon marjoram

½ teaspoon oregano

¼ cup tomato paste

¼ cup guajillo purée (recipe follows)

1 tablespoon chipotle purée (recipe above)

4 cups chicken stock (or water with 2 teaspoons of sea salt)

1 tablespoon cornstarch mixed with ½ cup cold water

Sauté the onions and garlic in the olive oil for 10 minutes over medium heat until they start to turn light brown. While they are cooking, lightly brown the chiles under the top broiler of the oven.

Add the spices to the onions and cook for 2 to 3 minutes. Add the tomato paste and cook for 5 minutes over low heat. Add the remaining ingredients, except the cornstarch mixture, and bring the sauce to a boil. Simmer for 15 minutes before adding the cornstarch mixture. Stir and simmer for 5 minutes.

BARRIO GUACAMOLE

Barrio Café, Phoenix

[serves four]

1 Haas avocado, ripe

¼ serrano or jalapeño pepper, finely diced

2 tablespoons red onion, finely diced

2 tablespoons tomato, finely diced

1 tablespoon cilantro, julienned

¼ teaspoon kosher salt, or to taste

½ lime, juiced

2 tablespoons pomegranate seeds

Cut the avocado in half lengthwise, removing the pit. Score avocado half into cubes. Remove the avocado cubes from skin into a bowl by using a tablespoon.

Add the other ingredients, with the exception of the pomegranate seeds, and slightly toss, being careful not to bruise the avocado cubes.

Top with pomegranate seeds, to taste.

HUSH PUPPIES

Rancho de los Caballeros, Wickenburg

[makes 20 hush puppies]

1 + ½ cups all-purpose flour
1 + ½ cups cornmeal
2 tablespoons baking powder
2 tablespoons sugar
1 tablespoon baking soda
2 teaspoons kosher salt
½ teaspoon cayenne
1 + ½ cups buttermilk
2 eggs
1 yellow onion, grated
2 apples, cooked
2 quarts oil

Whisk together the flour, cornmeal, baking powder, sugar, baking soda, salt and cayenne.

In a separate bowl, combine the buttermilk, eggs, onion and apples. Pour over the dry ingredients and stir until just combined. Allow to rest for 1 hour.

In a 5-quart pot, heat 2 quarts of oil to 330 degrees. Use a deep-fryer thermometer and adjust the flame/heat to maintain temperature.

Line a large plate with paper towels to absorb excess grease from the hush puppies. Using two tablespoons, lightly dip the spoons in the hot oil, then scoop a tablespoon of dough and gently release it into the hot oil.

Remove the cooked hush puppies and place them on the paper-lined plate. Continue the process until all the hush puppies are cooked.

SCREAMING STIX

Screaming Banshee, Bisbee

[serves four]

All-purpose flour for dusting
8-ounce ball pizza dough, thawed if frozen
Extra-virgin olive oil for drizzling
Herbed garlic butter (recipe follows)
½ cup fresh mozzarella cheese (optional)
Parmesan-Asiago cheese blend, grated
Fresh parsley, chopped
Ranch or marinara sauce

Put a pizza stone into the oven and heat the oven to 500 degrees, allowing at least 30 minutes for the stone to warm.

On a floured surface, roll or stretch the dough to an oblong shape, about 9 by 12 inches. Transfer the dough to a floured pizza peel. Lightly drizzle olive oil over the dough. With a fork, poke holes over the surface of the dough and coat the dough with a layer of the garlic butter. If you would like to add cheese, add it at this time.

Slide the dough onto the stone and bake for about 4 minutes, until lightly golden and bubbling. Carefully spin the pizza on the stone and bake for 2 minutes longer, until the crust is browned. Slide onto a work surface, and sprinkle the surface with grated Parmesan-Asiago cheese blend and fresh chopped parsley. Cut into even strips and stack on plate. Serve with hot marinara or ranch sauce for dipping.

HERBED GARLIC BUTTER

1 teaspoon garlic, minced
1 teaspoon oregano
1 teaspoon basil
¼ teaspoon onion powder
¼ teaspoon lemon juice
¼ teaspoon sea salt
2 sticks unsalted butter, softened

Blend the herbs, lemon juice and salt in a food processor. Add them to the butter and mix.

DESSERTS

YUM YUM BOMBS

Blue Buddha Sushi Lounge, Page

[servings vary]

1 cup flour
1 tablespoon cornstarch
Pinch of salt
½ teaspoon vanilla extract
½ teaspoon cinnamon
1 + ½ cups soda water
3 cups vegetable oil
1 package Double Stuf Oreos
Vanilla ice cream
Chocolate sauce, melted

Combine flour, cornstarch, salt, vanilla extract, cinnamon and soda water to create a tempura batter. Mix gently, as you want the batter to be slightly runny.

Heat vegetable oil on medium-high.

When vegetable oil is ready, drop Oreos into tempura-batter mix, then tempura-fry until they're a light-golden color. This should take less than a minute.

Plate tempura-fried Oreos, and place one scoop of vanilla ice cream on top of each one. Drizzle the melted chocolate sauce on top.

MISS FIGGY CHEESECAKE

Cucina Rustica, Sedona

1 pound cream cheese

1 cup goat cheese

4 tablespoons heavy cream

1 cup Dalmatia Croatian fig spread or other marmalade or fig jam

2 tablespoons orange zest (optional)

3 eggs

½ cup granulated sugar

½ cup sour cream

3 ounces heavy cream

Preheat oven to 350 degrees.

Whip cream cheese, goat cheese and cream in the bowl of a food processor. Scrape into a mixing bowl with a spatula and fold in the fig jam. Be careful to not over-mix, leaving striations of the marmalade visible in the cheese. Feather in the zest.

Add eggs, sugar, sour cream and heavy cream. Mix until smooth, then pour the mixture into your favorite crust in a 9- or 10-inch springform pan. Bake in a water bath for 30 minutes. Turn down to 300 degrees for another 30 minutes. Let cool, then refrigerate for at least 3 hours.

GARLAND'S APPLE TART

Garland's Oak Creek Lodge, Sedona

[serves 12]

CRUST

3 cups all-purpose, unbleached flour

1 teaspoon salt

2 tablespoons sugar

12 tablespoons (6 ounces or 1 + ½ sticks) unsalted butter, cut into bits

10 tablespoons vegetable shortening

¼ cup cold water

1 tablespoon cider vinegar

FILLING

1 cup sour cream

¾ cup sugar

2 tablespoons unbleached flour

½ teaspoon salt

2 teaspoons vanilla

1 teaspoon cinnamon

1 egg

4 large cooking apples, peeled and sliced ¼-inch thick

STREUSEL

¾ cup flour

1 cup brown sugar

½ cup butter, cold and in cubes

To make the crust, combine the dry ingredients in a medium bowl and whisk lightly to blend. Add butter and shortening, toss lightly to just coat the pieces, then cut in with pastry cutter until mixture looks like a very coarse meal. Some fat pieces will look like small beans.

Mix water and vinegar together, then sprinkle about 3 tablespoons over the mixture. Toss together to blend. Add another tablespoon and toss together to form a ball. You may need more water to form a cohesive ball — add it a tablespoon at a time. Your dough should hold together when pressed, and it's better to not have it too dry. Form into 2 balls, flatten the balls into fattish discs, wrap and chill at least 2 hours. This is necessary to rest and relax the gluten in the flour and completely chill all the fats in the mixture.

For the filling, whisk the sour cream, sugar, flour, salt, vanilla, cinnamon and egg together until very smooth.

Add apple slices to the bowl, mix in gently, then set aside while preparing the tart shell.

Preheat oven to 375 degrees.

Divide dough into two pieces. Roll out one piece on a lightly floured surface to approximately ⅛ to ¼ inch in thickness. Trim edges into a large circle. Fold dough in half gently, then transfer to a 10-inch shallow, fluted, removable-bottom tart

pan. Place over half the pan, then unfold the dough, pressing in the bottom and sides to fit cleanly. With kitchen shears, cut the excess edge of the dough, leaving a scant ⅓ inch above the rim of the pan. Simply fold this down slightly, so it sits on the edge of the pan. Place pan in the freezer for 5 minutes.

Take the other piece of dough, press it gently into a disc, wrap it very well and freeze for another use. Or you can roll it out now, fit it into a pie or tart pan, wrap and freeze for later.

For the streusel, combine the flour and brown sugar in a food processor. Pulse to blend. Add butter cubes and pulse to cut in butter until a coarse meal is formed.

Transfer to a small bowl.

Take tart shell from the freezer. Spoon in the apples, spreading them evenly, then scrape in any additional sauce that's left in the bowl.

Bake in the lower third of the oven for 20 to 25 minutes, until the filling is just beginning to set. Pull from the oven and spread streusel over the apples, taking care to cover completely but within the rim of pastry. Place back in the oven, lower the temperature to 350 degrees and continue baking until a deep golden brown, 20 to 30 minutes more.

Cool on a rack for 30 minutes before cutting into 12 wedges. Serve with vanilla ice cream.

SOPAPILLAS

Santiago's, Bisbee

[serves six to eight]

2 cups all-purpose flour
2 teaspoons baking powder
1 tablespoon sugar
1 teaspoon salt
2 tablespoons shortening
¾ cup warm water, plus more as needed
Oil for frying
Honey, powdered sugar or cinnamon, for plating

Sift the dry ingredients together in a large mixing bowl. Add the shortening and water, then work them in with your hands to make a soft, pliable dough. Add more water, 1 teaspoon at a time, if the dough feels too dry. Gather the dough into a ball and wrap in plastic wrap. Put the dough in the refrigerator and chill for at least 1 hour so it will firm up and be easier to roll and cut.

Unwrap the ball of dough and put it on a lightly floured surface, sliced in half. With a floured rolling pin, roll each piece of dough into a circle, about ¼ inch thick. Using a paring knife, cut the dough into triangles. You should end up with 6 triangles per circle.

Heat oil to 375 degrees in the fryer.

Fry a few of the sopapillas at a time, keeping an eye on maintaining the oil temperature. As the sopapillas puff up and rise to the surface, flip them over with a slotted spoon. Serve hot with honey, powdered sugar or cinnamon.

PUMPKIN FLAN

Elote Café, Sedona

[serves four]

2 cups sugar (for flan mold)

6 eggs

6 egg yolks

2 cups half-and-half

1 teaspoon vanilla

1 teaspoon ground canela (cinnamon)

½ can sweetened condensed milk

½ can pumpkin-pie mix

Pinch of salt

Candied pumpkin seeds and fresh whipped cream
for garnish

Melt the sugar in a saucepan over medium-high heat until liquefied. Continue cooking and stir with a metal spoon until lightly browned and nutty-smelling. Use extreme caution and pour enough into individual ramekins to coat the bottom of the dish; then, quickly, while the caramel is still hot, swirl it to get the ramekin coated on the sides as well. Set aside to cool.

Preheat oven to 350 degrees.

Mix eggs, egg yolks, half-and-half, vanilla, canela, condensed milk and pumpkin-pie mix to make flan mixture.

Once cooled, place the ramekins into a baking pan, then fill the pan with water halfway up the sides of the ramekins. Fill the dishes with the flan mixture and bake for approximately 45 minutes or until the custard is set. Refrigerate for 4 hours or up to 3 days.

Unmold by taking a knife around the edge of the custard and inverting it onto a plate. Serve with candied pumpkin seeds and fresh whipped cream.

MUD PIE

Molly Butler Lodge, Greer

[serves eight]

24 Oreo cookies
¼ cup melted butter
Hot fudge, chilled
Coffee ice cream
Caramel, chocolate and white-chocolate syrup

Blend the Oreo cookies in a food processor until their texture is coarse. Add melted butter and blend until well combined. Place crumb mixture into a 9-inch deep-dish pie pan and press down until even on the bottom and sides. Put pie crust into freezer for about 2 hours.

When crust is frozen, spread cold fudge across the bottom, then fill with coffee ice cream. Let freeze another hour. To serve, top with whipped cream and syrup of your choice.

CRÈME BRÛLÉE

The Turquoise Room at La Posada, Winslow

[serves 12 to 16]

4 cups heavy cream
1 vanilla bean, cut lengthwise
10 egg yolks
¼ cup + 2 tablespoons sugar

Heat the cream with the vanilla bean in a thick-bottomed saucepan until it starts to boil. Remove from the heat and let stand for a few minutes. Meanwhile, place the yolks in a stainless-steel or glass bowl and add the ¼ cup sugar. Remove the vanilla bean from the cream and scrape out all of the black seeds before returning the seeds to the cream. Gradually stir the vanilla-infused cream into the egg mixture.

Place a pot on the stove with water and bring it to a boil. Make sure the bowl you are using fits over the top of the pot without dropping into it.

Reduce to a slow boil and place the bowl on top of the pot. Use a whisk and a plastic spatula to stir the mixture so that it does not scramble. This is the most difficult part, and it will take about 30 minutes before the mixture becomes thick and coats the back of the spatula. The temperature of the mixture should be 170 degrees. When it is cooked, strain it through a fine strainer, pour into ramekins and place into the refrigerator so they will set. Caramelizing the sugar topping takes place just before serving.

Pour a thin and even layer of the sugar on top of the custard, about ⅛ inch thick. Use a propane torch with a soft flame, and hold it 4 to 8 inches away from the sugar. Move the flame over the dish constantly until the sugar starts to melt and brown. Let cool for 5 minutes and serve with fresh berries.

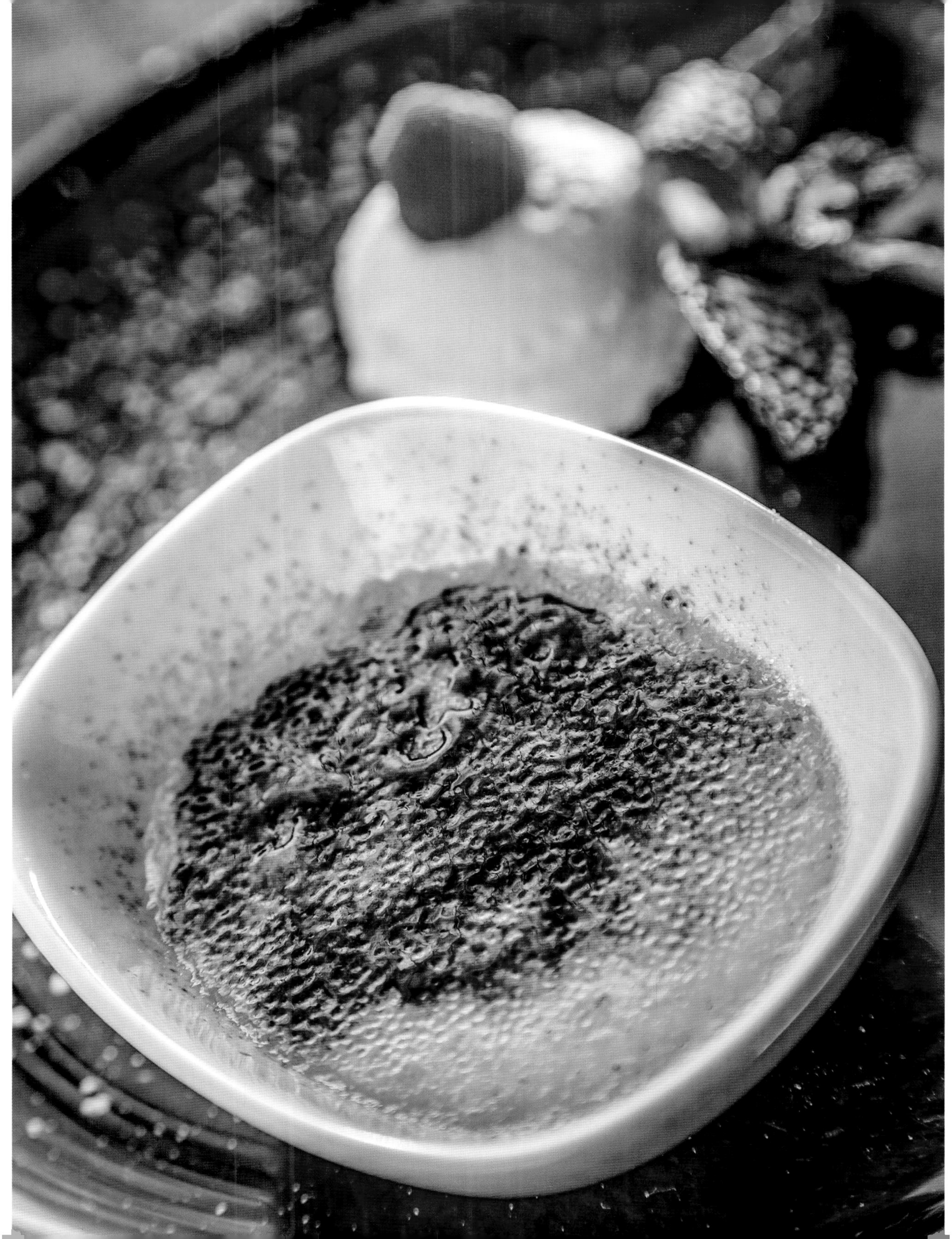

POPCORN SEMIFREDDO

Brix, Flagstaff

[serves four]

3 tablespoons popcorn kernels
3 tablespoons butter, melted
2 tablespoons kosher salt
4 cups heavy whipping cream
1 cup sugar
6 egg yolks
1 teaspoon pure vanilla extract

Use any method of your choosing to pop the popcorn kernels.

In large kitchen bowl, season the popcorn with butter and salt. Add popcorn to the heavy cream and soak it overnight. Strain popcorn from cream with a fine sieve and reserve cream.

Measure out 2 + ½ cups of popcorn cream. In a mixer with a whisk attachment, whisk the cream into medium peaks.

Add ½ cup of the sugar to the cream and continue to whisk until stiff peaks form. Turn the cream out into a large bowl. Clean the bowl and whisk attachment.

Add the egg yolks and the remaining ½ cup sugar. Whisk until the yolks are pale yellow and tripled in volume. Add the yolks to the whipped cream.

Add the vanilla extract and begin to fold the yolks into the cream.

Turn the mixture out into a glass serving dish. Freeze overnight. Serve with salted caramel, popped popcorn or both.

SPICED VENEZUELAN CHOCOLATE CAKE

Criollo Latin Kitchen, Flagstaff

[serves 10]

¾ cup brewed decaf coffee

1 cup granulated sugar

¾ pound dark chocolate (72 percent cacao)

1 + ¼ cup butter

1 tablespoon chile powder

½ teaspoon cayenne pepper

½ teaspoon ground cinnamon

4 large eggs

Preheat oven to 350 degrees. Spray 10 4-ounce ramekins with pan spray. Arrange on a cookie sheet and set aside.

In a small saucepan, bring the coffee and ¼ cup sugar to a boil. Lower heat to a simmer, and reduce mixture by half (½ cup). Set aside.

In a double boiler over low heat, melt the chocolate and butter together. Stir occasionally to keep the chocolate from scorching. Once the mixture is smooth, add your coffee reduction and stir.

In a small bowl, stir together the chile powder, cayenne pepper and ground cinnamon. Sprinkle this over the chocolate mixture and stir until combined.

In a large bowl, whisk together the eggs and remaining sugar. Whip this mixture until it begins to turn a pale yellow and the sugar has dissolved completely. While whisking the egg mixture, slowly drizzle in your spiced chocolate mixture. Mix until combined. Pour this mixture into your prepared ramekins.

Bake for 6 minutes. Carefully rotate the pan and bake an additional 6 to 8 minutes, or until cakes are mostly set with the centers slightly wet. Remove from the oven and allow to cool. Serve with vanilla-bean ice cream or Chantilly cream.

LEMON BARS

Pangaea Bakery, Prescott

[serves 20]

SHORTBREAD BASE
4 cups all-purpose flour
1 cup granulated sugar
1 pound unsalted butter

FILLING
4 cups granulated sugar
¾ cup all-purpose flour
¾ teaspoon baking powder
8 eggs
1 tablespoon lemon extract (optional)
1 cup fresh squeezed lemon juice
Powdered sugar, sifted
Preheat oven to 375 degrees.

Combine the flour and sugar in the bowl of a mixer with a paddle attachment and blend on low speed to combine well. Add the butter to the bowl all at once and mix on medium speed until combined well.

Turn out the shortbread mixture onto a lightly greased half sheet pan lined with a sheet of parchment paper. Press evenly into the pan, including edges and corners. Bake for approximately 20 minutes until golden brown.

To make the filling, add all the dry ingredients to a large bowl. Add the eggs, lemon extract and lemon juice and whisk to combine well.

After the shortbread has baked completely, remove from oven and pour the filling directly into the hot shortbread in the pan. Return to oven and bake for 25 to 35 minutes longer, until the entire lemon filling moves only slightly when you shake the pan.

Remove from oven and let cool completely. Sprinkle with sifted powdered sugar.

FRUIT BURRITO

Wisdom's Café, Tumacacori

[makes one burrito]

1 thin flour tortilla
¾ cup fruit pie filling
Vegetable or canola oil for frying
Sugar and cinnamon for rolling

Take a flour tortilla, the thinner the better, and put the fruit filling of your choice right in the middle. Roll up into a burrito and secure the ends with toothpicks. To make it really easy, just choose a delicious pie filling such as apple or peach.

Once you've secured the ends of the tortilla, drop the burrito into a pot of vegetable or canola oil and deep-fry until golden and crispy. Let the burrito drain for a few minutes and then, while still hot, roll it in a mixture of equal parts sugar and cinnamon.

Cut in half and serve with a scoop of vanilla ice cream.

VANILLA RICE PUDDING

Maynards Market and Kitchen, Tucson

[serves 15]

2 + ½ cups jasmine rice, parboiled with 3 cups water
3 cups sugar
4 cans coconut milk
3 cups cream
3 cups whole milk
2 split vanilla beans

Boil the rice with water, then add all other ingredients once the water has evaporated. Stir frequently on low heat until the rice has achieved a pudding-like texture. Pour rice into hotel pan and place plastic wrap directly onto the rice to prevent a skin from forming. Cool before serving.

This versatile pudding can be served with compressed pineapple, deep-fried pastry cream or any number of other additions.

BREAD PUDDING WITH MIXED-BERRY CREAM SAUCE

Pangaea Bakery, Prescott

[serves 18]

8 eggs

2 egg yolks

1 + ½ cups sugar

4 + ½ cups whole milk

5 cups heavy cream

¼ cup bourbon or brandy (optional)

2 teaspoons vanilla

1 teaspoon nutmeg

⅛ teaspoon salt

2 + ½ pounds bread, cubed (for a richer pudding, substitute stale pastries such as croissants or cinnamon rolls for 1 pound of the bread)

Whisk together all ingredients except bread in a large bowl. Add cubed bread and push down to absorb. Let sit in refrigerator for 8 hours to absorb liquid.

Preheat oven to 375 degrees.

Press into a buttered 16-inch-square pan that's 2 or 3 inches high. Bake 50 minutes or until top springs back when lightly pressed.

The batter can also be scooped into large muffin tins and baked for individual dessert servings.

Top with Mixed-Berry Cream Sauce or any topping of your choice.

MIXED-BERRY CREAM SAUCE

1 cup water

1 cup sugar

2 teaspoons ground ginger

1 cup ripe berries (raspberries, blueberries, strawberries, blackberries, any mix)

4 cups heavy cream

Place water and sugar into a medium saucepan. Bring to a boil and reduce to simmer. Add ginger and cook until sugar is dissolved. Add fruit to sugar mixture and cook until fully softened. Take off heat and cool.

In a saucepan, add heavy cream and bring to a simmer over medium-high heat. Pan should be large enough to allow room for cream expansion. Stir occasionally. Do not let hot cream go over top of pan. Reduce cream by about 50 percent. Add fruit mixture and stir. Take off heat and blend until smooth with either an immersion blender or regular blender. Keep refrigerated when not in use.

BISBEE BERRY PIE

Bisbee Breakfast Club, Bisbee

[serves six]

5 cups mixed berries (strawberries, blackberries, raspberries, blueberries)
Juice of 1 lemon
1 cup sugar
¼ cup cornstarch
1 unbaked pie shell
½ cup oats
¼ cup flour
¼ cup brown sugar
¼ cup almonds, blanched and chopped
¾ cup butter, grated
½ teaspoon cinnamon
Dash of nutmeg

Preheat oven to 370 degrees.

Combine berries, lemon juice and sugar in a large pot. Heat gently over low heat, stirring constantly, until the berries have released some of their juices but still maintain their shape and the sugar has dissolved. Remove from heat.

Add cornstarch and mix well. Transfer mixture to 9-inch unbaked pie shell. Cover pie with "oatly nutly" topping (oats, flour, brown sugar, almonds, butter, cinnamon and nutmeg) and spray lightly with cooking oil.

Bake for 35 minutes.

Let cool to room temperature for 1 hour, then refrigerate. Serve warm with a scoop of vanilla ice cream.

FRENCH CHOCOLATE AND SEA SALT CARAMEL TART

Essence Bakery Café, Tempe and Phoenix

[serves eight]

DOUGH

10 ounces butter, room temperature
¾ cup powdered sugar, sifted
1 teaspoon salt
1 teaspoon vanilla extract
2 eggs
3 + ¼ cups all-purpose flour, sifted
¼ cup cocoa powder, sifted
¼ cup almond meal
Chocolate tart shells

Soften butter; do not cream. Add sugar, salt and vanilla, and combine. Add eggs. Combine flour, cocoa powder and almond meal. Add to mixture just to combine — do not over-mix. Cover with plastic wrap and allow to rest at least 2 hours. Freezes well. Bake shell at 325 degrees for 10 to 12 minutes.

CARAMEL SAUCE

2 cups sugar
1 cup water
3 cups heavy cream

In a heated saucepan, use whisk to combine sugar and water. Stop stirring and wet down sides of pan with moistened brush. Repeat wetting sides of pan with brush to push down any sugar crystals to melt. Continue cooking until dark-amber color. While sugar is cooking, heat cream in separate saucepan. When sugar has reached desired color, remove from heat and very slowly pour a ladleful of hot cream onto caramel. (Mixture will spatter; be careful, it's very hot.) Whisk hot cream into caramel little by little, making sure to stir well between each addition.

CHOCOLATE GANACHE

2 cups heavy cream
1 pound dark chocolate
1 ounce butter, softened

Heat cream and pour over dark chocolate. Stir to melt chocolate, and add butter little by little.

Pour into baked chocolate tart shells lined with caramel and sea salt.

THE RESTAURANTS

For more from each of the restaurants included in this cookbook, visit them at the following locations, which, at press time, were accurate.

The Asylum | 200 Hill Street, Jerome | 928-639-3197 | www.theasylum.biz

Barrio Café | 2814 N. 16th Street, Phoenix | 602-636-0240 | www.barriocafe.com

Bisbee Breakfast Club | 75A Erie Street, Bisbee | 520-432-5885 | www.bisbeebreakfastclub.com

Blue Buddha Sushi Lounge | 644 N. Navajo Drive, Page | 928-645-0007 | www.bluebuddhasushi.com

Brix | 413 N. San Francisco Street, Flagstaff | 928-213-1021 | www.brixflagstaff.com

Cafe Roka | 35 Main Street, Bisbee | 520-432-5153 | www.caferoka.com

Caffe Torino Ristorante Italiano | 10325 N. La Cañada Drive, Tucson | 520-297-3777 | www.caffetorinoorovalley.com

Cliff Dwellers Restaurant | Milepost 541.5, U.S. Route 89A, Marble Canyon | 928-355-2261 | www.cliffdwellerslodge.com

Cucina Rustica | 7000 State Route 179, Suite 126A, Sedona | 928-284-3010 | www.cucinarustica.com

Dara Thai Café | 145 W. Historic Route 66, Suite C, Williams | 928-635-2201

Diablo Burger | 120 N. Leroux Street, Flagstaff | 928-774-3274 | www.diabloburger.com

Elote Café | 771 State Route 179, Sedona | 928-203-0105 | www.elotecafe.com

El Tovar Dining Room | South Rim, Grand Canyon National Park | 928-638-2631

Enzo's Ristorante Italiano | 423 W. Snowflake Boulevard, Snowflake | 928-243-0450

Essence Bakery Café | 3830 E. Indian School Road, Phoenix | 602-296-4958 | www.essencebakery.com

Garland's Oak Creek Lodge | 8067 N. State Route 89A, Sedona | 928-282-3343 | www.garlandslodge.com

Gerardo's Firewood Café | 512 State Route 87, Payson | 928-468-6500

Josephine's | 503 N. Humphreys Street, Flagstaff | 928-779-3400 | www.josephinesrestaurant.com

Liberty Market | 230 N. Gilbert Road, Gilbert | 480-892-1900 | www.libertymarket.com

Manzanita Restaurant | 11425 E. Cornville Road, Cornville | 928-634-8851 | www.themanzanitarestaurant.com

Matt's Big Breakfast | 825 N. First Street, Phoenix | 602-254-1074 | www.mattsbigbreakfast.com

Maynards Market & Kitchen | 400 N. Toole Avenue, Tucson | 520-545-0577 | www.maynardstucson.com

Molly Butler Lodge | 109 Main Street, Greer | 928-735-7226 | www.mollybutlerlodge.com

Pangaea Bakery | 220 W. Goodwin Street, Prescott | 928-778-2953 | www.pangaeabakery.net

Rancho de los Caballeros | 1551 S. Vulture Mine Road, Wickenburg | 928-684-5484 | www.ranchodeloscaballeros.com

The Randall House | 3821 State Route 87, Pine | 928-476-4077 | www.therandallhouse.com

Santiago's | 1 Howell Avenue, Bisbee | 520-432-1910 | www.santiagosmexican.blogspot.com

Screaming Banshee | 200 Tombstone Canyon, Bisbee | 520-432-1300 | www.screamingbansheepizza.net

Sirens' Café | 419 E. Beale Street, Kingman | 928-753-4151 | www.sirensinkingman.com

Stables Ranch Grille | 1 Avenida de Otero, Tubac | 520-398-2678 | www.tubacgolfresort.com/dining.php

Tinderbox Kitchen | 34 S. San Francisco Street, Flagstaff | 928-226-8400 | www.tinderboxkitchen.com

Tucson Tamale Co. | 2545 E. Broadway Boulevard, Tucson | 520-305-4760 | www.tucsontamale.com

The Turquoise Room at La Posada | 305 E. Second Street, Winslow | 928-289-2888 | www.theturquoiseroom.net

Twisters 50s Soda Fountain | 417 E. Historic Route 66, Williams | 928-635-0266 | www.route66place.com

Wisdom's Café | 1931 E. Frontage Road, Tumacacori | 520-398-2397 | www.wisdomscafe.com

INDEX